BIG GAME. BIGGER IMPACT.

Big Game, Bigger Impact takes you behind the scenes for an insider's peek into how the power of sports can create positive change. Gallagher and Martin make a fascinating business case for corporate social impact. A must-read for any executive looking to grow their business in a community.

Larry Baer

CEO of the San Francisco Giants

Fittingly set in California's Bay Area, a destination synonymous with innovation and creativity, Super Bowl 50 redefined the consumer experience for large-scale sports and entertainment events. *Big Game, Bigger Impact* tells the compelling story of an effort that paid dividends for California.

Caroline Beteta

President & CEO, Visit California

There's nothing bigger than the Super Bowl. And there's never been anything bigger than the 50th anniversary of the Super Bowl. It takes a <u>real</u> village to pull off something like that—a village of public and private sector giants! *Big Game, Bigger Impact* provides a fascinating look into what it took to accomplish something as big as the golden anniversary Super

Bowl in a complicated city like San Francisco. It should be required reading for all organizers of world-class events.

Former San Francisco Mayor Willie L. Brown, Jr.

For Super Bowl 50, we established an ambitious goal of 'redefining' the Super Bowl experience. This book recounts the incredible story of how that all happened [during our three-year journey together]. Pat and Stephanie tell the inspiring story of how we accomplished our mission, and how the San Francisco Bay Area came together to ensure that Super Bowl 50 would set a new standard for global sporting events going forward.

Keith Bruce
CEO & President, San Francisco Bay Area Super Bowl 50 Host Committee

Big Game, Bigger Impact is the inspiring true story of how the San Francisco Bay Area community came together to redefine the Super Bowl experience. Pat Gallagher and Stephanie Martin shine a light on how amazing things can happen when people come together in partnership. This book is not only relevant for those looking at mega events, the lessons learned apply to those contemplating any business or community event or activity. Besides, it's an intriguing read that provides life lessons for all of us. I highly recommend it!

Joe D'Alessandro
President & CEO, San Francisco Travel

In *Big Game, Bigger Impact,* Pat Gallagher and Stephanie Martin tell of the amazing journey of bringing Super Bowl 50 to the Bay Area, after a 31-year drought. In the Bay Area, we set high expectations for anything we do. Not only is the story a great read, but along the way, Pat and Stephanie share how our community came together to deliver the most important Super Bowl to date. They tell the story of how it all happened, and the lessons learned that can be applied to any massive business endeavor.

Joe Davis
Senior Partner and Managing Director
Boston Consulting Group

Superbly crafted exposition of behind-the-scenes of a highly successful mega-event. Rich learnings for both sports management in general, and for the planning and the execution of complex events with multiple stakeholders and a global audience.

George Foster, Ph.D.
Konosuke Matsushita Professor of Management
Graduate School of Business Stanford University

Big Game, Bigger Impact outlines the gold standard of how a community thrives when we work together! As one of the $500,000 Game Changer Grant recipients from the Super Bowl 50 Fund, Fresh Lifelines for Youth (FLY) was able to expand and deepen our work with at-risk and system involved juvenile justice youth in the Bay Area. I see firsthand the impact Super Bowl 50 has on our community and am so grateful!

Christa Gannon
Founder & CEO, Fresh Lifelines for Youth (FLY)

Big Game, Bigger Impact is a blueprint for leveraging a large-scale event to create real, positive change. It was an honor to work alongside Pat Gallagher and Stephanie Martin on Super Bowl 50; it had a lasting impact well beyond the game ended, and their book chronicles that journey with thoughtful reflection. I'm hopeful this story will inspire future events to follow in our footsteps.

Daniel Lurie
CEO and Founder, Tipping Point
Chairman of the San Francisco Bay Area Super Bowl 50
Host Committee

In the San Francisco Bay Area, we constantly challenge the status quo and our approach to hosting a Super Bowl was no different. In *Big Game, Bigger Impact*, Pat Gallagher and Stephanie Martin pull back the curtain on how our community came together to show the world not only how a Super Bowl could be run, but also the kind of legacy it could create across our region.

Lt. Governor Gavin Newsom, State of California

Super Bowl 50 was a milestone event for the NFL. It was a year-long celebration that not only honored our past, but set the tone for the next 50 Super Bowls. Our vision required great partners and innovative ideas. The San Francisco Bay Area Super Bowl 50 Host Committee served as the unique partner we needed. In this book, Pat Gallagher and Stephanie Martin capture the spirit of this milestone year--how they captivated the region, navigated through challenges, and left a powerful, positive legacy across the entire Bay Area.

Peter O'Reilly
NFL Senior Vice President of Events

Big Game, Bigger Impact is the story of how the Super Bowl can be so much more than just the world's greatest sporting event. The authors Pat Gallagher and Stephanie Martin remind us how much can be accomplished when a community comes together to pursue a goal. They explain how the Bay Area formulated a winning game plan, executed it to near perfection and ultimately scored.

Carmen A. Policy
Napa Valley Vintner & Former President and CEO
of San Francisco 49ers

Big Game, Bigger Impact captures the essence of hosting a Super Bowl, from the day-to-day blocking and tackling to the strategies that can result in championship experiences for fans. Pat Gallagher and Stephanie Martin deliver an important read for anyone in international event management as well as a model for how events like the Super Bowl can make a real difference in their host communities.

Daniel Rascher, Ph.D., CVA
Professor & Director, Sport Management Program,
University of San Francisco
President of SportsEconomics, and Partner at OSKR

Pat Gallagher and Stephanie Martin take us behind the scenes to tell the story of how Super Bowl 50 broke new ground—engaging a region from Sonoma to San Jose, bringing millions to Super Bowl City in the middle of San Francisco, and creating a philanthropic legacy to support nonprofits across the Bay Area. Whether you're a veteran sports marketer, a business leader, or a fan who has always wondered what goes into making this huge sports event happen, you will enjoy and learn from *Big Game, Bigger Impact.*

Becky Saeger
Former CMO, Charles Schwab and EVP Marketing, Visa

I experienced firsthand the power of the Super Bowl 50 Host Committee's philanthropic efforts as the CEO of Juma Ventures, a recipient of the $500,000 Game Changers Award. The investment helped accelerate the impact we are making with low-income youth. *Big Game, Bigger Impact* reveals the thoughtful steps taken to ensure the community benefitted in a meaningful and lasting way!

Marc Spencer
CEO, Juma Ventures

With millions of dollars in economic impact and direct investments in local businesses and nonprofits, Super Bowl 50 is a real-life example of how global sporting events can leave a lasting legacy. Pat Gallagher and Stephanie Martin have taken the principles that established their solid professional records, and applied them to the biggest stage possible in America, the Super Bowl. In *Big Game, Bigger Impact*, the authors share the roadmap their organization followed and the moral compass that guided them.

Dr. William A. "Bill" Sutton
Founder and Director, Sport and Entertainment Business Graduate Program, University of South Florida
Principal, Bill Sutton & Associates

From our first meeting, it was clear that Pat and Stephanie were going to bring the best of the Bay Area to the Super Bowl and re-write the playbook along the way. *Big Game, Bigger Impact* brilliantly captures the exciting journey to Super Bowl 50, with anecdotes, behind-the-scenes stories and wisdom that both entertains you and makes you think. A must-read for innovative thinkers and sports fans alike.

Lorraine Twohill
SVP Marketing, Google

Whether or not you're a football fan, *Big Game, Bigger Impact*, is an inspirational must-read story for anyone wanting an insider play-by-play on how to give back to community, big time. Having first-hand experience working with the Host Committee, I saw the real impact they made on our nonprofit. Authors Pat Gallagher and Stephanie Martin bring you on the field and inside the board rooms with a fast-read, story-filled playbook with insights that anyone who wants to give back can learn from.

Villy Wang
Founder, President & CEO of BAYCAT
TED Speaker

To deliver the most spectacular Super Bowl to date, we knew cities throughout the San Francisco Bay Area had to come together in a way they never had before. The way our community galvanized not only exceeded expectations, but also resulted in a win for the entire region in making the event the most philanthropic Super Bowl ever. *Big Game, Bigger*

Impact provides not only the blueprint for how it was done, but also lessons that can benefit any business leader.

Jed York

CEO of the San Francisco 49ers

I was proud to be part of the Super Bowl 50 Host Committee effort and even more proud of how the Bay Area community put on a Super Bowl experience of a lifetime. In the Bay Area, we know a lot about being champions, and with Super Bowl 50, we had the chance to shine once again; (Host Committee CEO) Keith Bruce and I could attest to that. In *Big Game, Bigger Impact*, Pat Gallagher and Stephanie Martin share the story of how our community came together and set the bar for how all future Super Bowls should be experienced.

Steve Young

Pro Football Hall of Famer, 3-time Super Bowl Champion and Super Bowl XXIX MVP

BIG GAME BIGGER IMPACT

How the Bay Area Redefined the Super Bowl Experience
and the Lessons that Can Apply to Any Business

By Pat Gallagher
with Stephanie Martin

Motivational PRESS®
LEADERS IN GLOBAL PUBLISHING

Published by Motivational Press, Inc.
1777 Aurora Road
Melbourne, Florida, 32935
www.MotivationalPress.com

Copyright 2017 © by Pat Gallagher & Stephanie Martin
Photo credits: Christopher Dydyk, JJ Harris and Stephanie Martin

All Rights Reserved

No part of this book may be reproduced or transmitted in any form by any means: graphic, electronic, or mechanical, including photocopying, recording, taping or by any information storage or retrieval system without permission, in writing, from the authors, except for the inclusion of brief quotations in a review, article, book, or academic paper. The authors and publisher of this book and the associated materials have used their best efforts in preparing this material. The authors and publisher make no representations or warranties with respect to accuracy, applicability, fitness or completeness of the contents of this material. They disclaim any warranties expressed or implied, merchantability, or fitness for any particular purpose. The authors and publisher shall in no event be held liable for any loss or other damages, including but not limited to special, incidental, consequential, or other damages. If you have any questions or concerns, the advice of a competent professional should be sought.

Manufactured in the United States of America.

ISBN: 978-1-62865-409-7

CONTENTS

This book is dedicated to every person who made Super Bowl 50 possible. While it is impossible to recognize you all individually, please know that your contributions were the inspiration for this book.

Personally, we'd also like to show our gratitude for:

My friend Bill Campbell for his wisdom and coaching, even now from the other side, and my wife Joan for everything else.

-P.G.

My parents, Linda and Bob, for teaching me to believe anything is possible, and my husband Mike for bringing such joy to my life every day.

-S.M.

THE BAY AREA MADE ME WHO I AM.

I am proud of my origins, born and bred in the South Bay to a loving family who were always in my corner. We may not have been wealthy, but we were rich in so many other ways: a tight-knit community of family and friends, a shared pride of our Mexican-American heritage and most importantly, an abundance of love. It was my family's love that gave me the confidence to believe I could do anything I set my mind on.

I had the opportunity to play football at James Lick High School in East San Jose and Stanford University, with amazing teammates who became devoted friends, people with whom I've been friends for now decades. I hold those eight years dearly in my heart, and love still being an active member of the Stanford football community with my wife Gerry and supporting our next generations of young players.

After beginning my career at the New England Patriots, I had the opportunity to come home to my friends and family, playing for the San Francisco 49ers and finally finishing my career at the Oakland Raiders. The Raiders gave me the chance to not only stay in the Bay Area, but also to become a champion. I couldn't be more proud that my greatest professional accomplishments took place in the region I love so much, the place that made me the person I am today.

It is because of this love that I got involved with the San Francisco Bay Area Super Bowl 50 Host Committee. In 2016, the Bay Area had the opportunity to host its first Super Bowl in more than 30 years and in my mind, there was no better place to hold the 50th celebration of professional football's biggest prize. I had no doubt that the Bay Area would shine on this global stage, but I also knew this opportunity could mean more to the region than just the game.

The Host Committee's approach rang true to me, using this opportunity to not only set a new bar for how Super Bowls are hosted, but to ensure an event of this magnitude would leave a real legacy of good for the Bay Area. When they shared that they wanted Super Bowl 50 to be the most giving Super Bowl yet, I knew that was a record I wanted to help set.

Over the course of two years, I was incredibly inspired to see how our region came together, from San Francisco to Sacramento to Santa Clara and everywhere in between. Cities, communities, nonprofits, corporations, small businesses, volunteers, you name it. Thousands of people across the Bay Area worked together to make Super Bowl 50 the success that it was.

I also saw firsthand the Host Committee team at work – they worked as hard as any championship professional football team. It wasn't just the hours and effort they put in, but more importantly, the way that they approached this work: with a dogged focus on inclusion and respect for every stakeholder, and ensuring a legacy of positive impact would be realized. They wanted everyone in the Bay Area to feel invited to the celebration, and I felt the positive reaction to this warm welcome every time I interacted with fans, supporters and volunteers.

My favorite personal memory was having the opportunity to return to James Lick High School with my teammate Phil Passifuime and give the school a commemorative Golden Football as part of the NFL's High School Honor Roll program. It felt great walking into that gym, speaking to the student body and being able to say thank you once again to the school that helped define my professional life.

The making of Super Bowl 50 was an extraordinary experience that I'm happy to say is detailed in the following pages of this book. Pat Gallagher and Stephanie Martin's book provides not only an insider's account into this inner world of hosting Super Bowls, but also serves as an important reminder about how much can be accomplished when a community comes together. *Big Game, Bigger Impact* is a must for anyone who wants to be a game changer, whether they work in sports or not.

The hosting of Super Bowl 50 has made me proud to say, once again, that I am from the Bay Area. Super Bowl 50 proved that a sporting event could make lasting contributions to its host community. Our celebration had a real impact on the sport of professional football, and our approach is a model that I hope will be replicated many times over.

**-Jim Plunkett, two-time Super Bowl Champion
and Super Bowl XV MVP; Heisman Trophy winner;
and San Francisco Bay Area Super Bowl 50
Host Committee Legends Member**

PREFACE

May 21, 2013. Boston Longwharf Marriott.

Months of planning and preparing had all come down to this moment, and no one had any idea what was going to happen next.

Together, we sat in a windowless conference room that served as our holding pen while the big show went on in the Grand Ballroom. Twenty-four hours of practice and pulling it together—both the presentation and our nerves—were now over, and all we could do was wait for a signal from NFL officials. Who was going to win the opportunity to host the 50th or 51st Super Bowl was anyone's guess.

Our on-the-ground team included San Francisco Bid Committee Chair Daniel Lurie and bid coordinator Danielle DeLancey, Steve Van Dorn of the Santa Clara Convention & Visitor's Bureau, Michael Crain and Luke Dillon from ad agency Goodby Silverstein & Partners, SF Travel head honcho Joe D'Alessandro and me. My role was to secure the corporate backing that would show our region's commitment to hosting a Super Bowl. Thanks to a few of our region's business leaders and an assist from legendary Silicon Valley advisor, coach and my good friend Bill Campbell, we were coming to the table with about $30 million in pledges.

Our group—the San Francisco Bid Committee—had the hope of bringing the 50th Super Bowl home, but truthfully, we would have been happy with either game. The Super Bowl hadn't been in the Bay Area since the "dark ages" of 1985 when it was held at the old Stanford Stadium. It's been said that legendary NFL owner Lamar Hunt—the man who coined the term "Super Bowl"—got splinters in his backside from the stadium's wooden bench seats and muttered to his wife: "we are never coming back here!" And never back had the Super Bowl come.

Hours earlier, we were shown to our war room, which was sandwiched in between our two more experienced competitors, South Florida and Houston. We were up against South Florida for Super Bowl L, and the loser of the first round would go up against Houston for Super Bowl LI. We had the opportunity to win one, or none.

The experience and confidence of the Houston and South Florida bid teams were obvious from the onset. In the hallway outside our war rooms was extensive catering for both cities, both of which had hosted Super Bowls in the past decade. We had a tray of water and soft drinks. We didn't have the money to afford much more and, frankly, we were too nervous to eat.

We set up our room with a few tourism posters and our bid logo that featured the Golden Gate Bridge as football goal posts. We also had a 49ers helmet for decoration, which provided us with some comic relief as the waiting dragged on. Fortunately, the photos of me with that helmet on haven't made the light of day yet.

To our mild horror, there was one consistent feature in all the rooms: NFL Network cameras and sound equipment, set up to capture each group's reaction to who had won and who had lost. Looking at the cameras, I thought to myself: "How cool is this?" It was a reminder that what we were doing was important enough to be on live television. But it was also a reminder that if we screwed this up, it would be there for the world to see. This moment really meant something to the many people back home who helped us get to this point. We tried not to think about it as we tweaked and practiced our final pitch. The NFL production team assured us that there was a few seconds' delay, and content would be sanitized of any expletives before going on the air.

Earlier in the day, we got the opportunity to practice in the actual ballroom where we would do our final presentation. The room was set with two long tables running perpendicular to the presentation stage. These tables were really long because we were presenting to not only the 32 club owners, but also their representatives and League officials; several hundred high-backed black leather swivel chairs lined each side. Commissioner Roger Goodell and senior NFL officials would be seated at a long dais at the front of the room. The two massive video screens above the stage and assorted monitors scattered throughout the room provided the only light, while dozens of cameras were strategically placed to capture absolutely everything.

About 30 minutes prior to our presentation, we were led into a staging area just outside the ballroom. The South Florida delegation was up first, and we could hear the high points of their presentation punctuated with music and deep bass through the walls. Suddenly, the doors opened and five of us—Daniel, Joe, Steve, Danielle and I—were ushered into the room.

It was an intimidating scene to say the least. Pitch-black except for the monitors, you could sense the weightiness of the moment in the room. Several hundred of the wealthiest people in the world were staring back at us, in complete silence. I felt like we were about to elect a new Pope.

All we could do now was watch and listen as Daniel and Joe made our case for a San Francisco Bay Area Super Bowl. Months of preparation had come down to a 15-minute pitch. As the guys finished, we stared across the giant room that was now deafeningly silent; our presentation didn't receive a single reaction. Were we any good? Did we blow it? We had no way to know as NFL officials led us back to our war room.

Once inside, we hugged each other, and then just sat and waited. Finally, we got word that Houston had finished their presentation, a moment that triggered the monitors in our room to come alive and show us the view from the ballroom. As our phones buzzed with well wishes, we sat and watched the voting unfold right before our eyes.

After a very short time, we were notified the owners had reached a decision. There was no more time left to wait, so we just stared at the monitors in the room and watched as a League official passed a slip of paper to the Commissioner on the dais. Commissioner Goodell cleared his throat and began to read into the microphone. "It gives me great pleasure to announce that the 50th Super Bowl, Super Bowl L, is awarded to...San Francisco."

We burst into cheers and leapt in the air, hugging and high-fiving, completely forgetting that all our movements were being broadcast on live television. Our mobile phones literally exploded with texts, tweets, emails and calls. Next door, the NFL Network broadcasted the silence in the South Florida war room. The thrill of victory and agony of defeat, side by side, in real-time.

The door suddenly swung open, and Commissioner Goodell and 49ers CEO Jed York strode in with NFL vice president of special events Frank Supovitz, all smiles, handshakes and hugs. Somebody opened a bottle of champagne. Don Lockerbie, a member of the South Florida delegation and a friend from my days with the San Francisco Giants, walked in with two bottles of wine for us to toast our victory. It was a classy move. They still had hopes of being awarded the 51st Super Bowl, so we wished them well.

We were then asked to meet with members of the press who were waiting down the hall to report the verdict. It was fun to share the excitement of the moment with the national and Bay Area reporters in attendance as celebrations were already happening back home.

Soon we learned Houston had been awarded the 51st game, so we made our way next door to hug and congratulate them as well. The South Florida green room was now empty except for the catering set-up in the hall; they were already making their way home after being shut out.

The next morning, waiting for our Virgin America flight back to San Francisco, the reality began to sink in. We had just been awarded a Super Bowl, and not just any Super Bowl. The 50th Super Bowl. The National Football League's Golden Anniversary. The biggest Super Bowl the NFL has ever celebrated. Now, we actually had to make it happen.

Holy shit.

INTRODUCTION

A nything presented live has irresistible drama. Will the team win or lose? Will anybody get hurt or worse? What will the real story be? Experts try to predict what will happen, but what makes these events so popular is the unpredictability. Nobody knows what will happen until it actually happens, and that's the beauty of it.

I've been fortunate to have always worked in the "fun business," but making things fun sure isn't as easy as it might appear. An event is sort of like an iceberg; the audience sees just the tiny tip above the surface, but never sees the years of planning or massive numbers of talented people who work enormous hours just below the surface. From my hourly summer job at Sea World to my senior management roles with the San Francisco Giants, I was hooked on this type of work. I loved being inside the iceberg, being behind-the-scenes and one of many pulling the strings to make it all happen. That is while keeping one eye out for the Titanic, of course.

Putting on the "show" is so much more than what you can see in front of you. Spectators, viewers and ticket buyers—our guests—just expect the game or the show to happen, like turning on a light switch. They don't necessarily appreciate the amount of time and talent it takes to make these spectaculars feel seamless and really, why should they? That's not their job, it's ours. We're the ones responsible for the planning, logistics, rehearsals and, eventually, the live execution. When it comes together as you hope and your guests leave satisfied with the value they received, there is no greater feeling of accomplishment. For me, there is nothing else quite like it.

During my many years in baseball, I would usually spend the majority of my time looking at the crowd in the stands rather than the game on the field. What were they doing? Were they paying attention? Were they falling asleep? Were they laughing and cheering, or booing and throwing things? Were they still there or had they left? Most importantly: did they think it was worth the time and money they invested? I couldn't impact the outcome of the game at all, but I could certainly help impact the quality of their experience. To me, what makes live entertainment so compelling is how you can combine showmanship and salesmanship to create something of real value for an audience. That was the true magic of being in the "fun business."

This was the way we approached Super Bowl 50. The game itself is the National Football League's annual big show. Our job as the Bay Area's Host Committee was to prepare the region to celebrate it, and deliver on everything promised in the bid presentation, including a legacy of good things for our local communities. Our challenge was figuring out how to create a superior overall Super Bowl experience, make our region proud to have been its host and, hopefully, give the Bay Area a chance to do it again. And to make this all come true, we needed a dedicated team of people and partners who could make it happen.

That is what this book is about: how a small band of like-minded Bay Area residents came together to not only host the world's single largest annual event, but also to give new meaning to the entire experience. Our team was successful because we built our Host Committee purposefully and upon a foundation of values that ultimately carried us to a record-setting Super Bowl, both on and off the field.

In writing this book, my co-author Stephanie Martin and I wanted to share not just what our organization did, but how we did it. Among stories from our two-year run-up to Super Bowl 50, we have highlighted the organizational values that drove us, as well as some of the lessons we learned along the way, lessons that we believe could benefit any business and, in particular, ones that are just starting up.

As you read, we will also subject you to some of my favorite tongue-in-cheek phrases in the form of chapter titles, little sayings that I would use around the office to the amusement or, more often, to rolling eyes of the rest of the team. Some just came to me and some I repurposed from other sources, but they made their way into our daily Host Committee vernacular. Because when you work in the "fun business," you might as well have some fun along the way.

THE EVOLUTION OF SUPER BOWL BIDDING

Major League Baseball, the NBA and the NHL give team owners and officials a chance to host championship games each year, but those championships games are held in the homes of those competing to hoist the trophy. The NFL is the only major professional sports league where the championship game is awarded to a neutral site years in advance.

The Super Bowl started out as a game to decide the champion of two rival leagues—the American Football League and the National Football League—as part of a merger agreement in the late 1960s. With the merger to be finalized in 1970, the two leagues agreed to hold a championship game to determine the world champion of American football starting in 1967. What began as the "AFL-NFL World Championship Game"—held at Los Angeles Memorial Coliseum with a halftime show featuring the University of Arizona and Grambling State University's marching bands, 300 pigeons and 10,000 balloons—has grown into a massive cultural phenomenon which attempts to out-do itself with each subsequent chapter.

After the first championship game under Commissioner Pete Rozelle, the NFL adopted a site rotation of sorts, which stayed in effect for the next 18 years. Aside from having a stadium big enough to host at least 70,000 fans, the League looked for warm-weather cities with picturesque surroundings that would televise well, such as Miami, New Orleans, Los Angeles, Pasadena, San Diego and Houston. As the popularity of the game increased in the late 70's and early 80's, the NFL allowed most any city, even cities without NFL teams, to bid. It was not unusual to have as many as 10 cities or more seeking to attract a Super Bowl to their area, which made the selection process cumbersome for the League.

For Super Bowl XIX, scheduled for January 1985, there were indeed 10 cities that wanted to play host. Bids came in from Pasadena, Miami, Seattle, Pontiac, Anaheim, Tampa, New Orleans, Jacksonville, Houston and San Francisco. Commissioner Rozelle reportedly had always wanted to award a game to San Francisco because of his long-standing affinity for the area that had developed when he worked at the University of San Francisco early in his career.

The main consideration in a bid during these times was having a suitable stadium to play the game. Though home to the San Francisco 49ers, Candlestick Park was never given serious consideration as a venue to include in a bid response, not only because of its capacity restraints but also because of its less-than-hospitable reputation and usual state of disrepair. As the longtime San Francisco Giants marketing and business guy, I knew the facility all too well. Each season, I tried almost anything to draw crowds to Candlestick Park for baseball games, but it was like trying to sell ice to the eskimos. Instead of Candlestick, nearby Stanford Stadium with its capacity of 85,500, was put forward in the bid as San Francisco's choice for Super Bowl XIX's host stadium, and at an NFL League meeting on December 14, 1982, San Francisco was awarded its very first Super Bowl.

Super Bowl XIX at Stanford Stadium in 1985 saw a series of firsts:

» It is the closest a home team had come to winning a Super Bowl. Local favorites Joe Montana and the San Francisco 49ers bested Dan Marino and the Miami Dolphins 38-16, but Stanford was not the 49ers' home stadium. As of Super Bowl 50, no home team had ever won the Lombardi Trophy at their home stadium.

» It was the first-time ABC broadcasted the game, which then joined the annual rotation with CBS and NBC, and later Fox.

» It was the first time a sitting US president participated in the coin toss. Ronald Reagan joined via satellite from the White House to toss the coin.

» It is the only time a Super Bowl stadium had wooden bench seats—then or since.

» It was the first time the fan experience spilled out of the stadium. There was a practical reason. Because its Palo Alto location was some 30 miles away from San Francisco and most of the hotel rooms, hospitality tents outside of the stadium gates provided ticket holders with a place to hang out before and after the game to ease transportation concerns.

Looking back, the 1985 Super Bowl was considered a turning point in the evolution of the process of awarding Super Bowls. From the hospitality tents around the stadium to creating public experiences in a host city, the seed was planted that a Super Bowl could potentially mean more to a host city and its residents than just the game itself.

JOINING THE BID COMMITTEE

It was in late September 2012 when San Francisco Travel President and CEO Joe D'Alessandro asked if I would meet him and someone named Daniel Lurie for a drink. He didn't tell me what it was about, but I knew Joe well enough to know it was something he considered important.

As a long-time board member and eventual chairman of San Francisco Travel (then called the San Francisco Convention and Visitor's Bureau), I met Joe when we recruited him to lead the organization in 2006. Through our work together, Joe and I became close friends and found that we shared similar business views. We both regarded what we did professionally as being in the "fun business."

As soon as we sat down in the lobby of the W Hotel in San Francisco, I recognized Daniel. An accomplished, entrepreneurial young man with extensive local family roots, he was someone who seemed to have cracked the code on effective philanthropy with Tipping Point, the high-impact anti-poverty organization he founded. And now he was leading the effort to try and bring another Super Bowl to the San Francisco Bay Area, tapped by San Francisco Mayor Ed Lee and 49ers CEO Jed York.

Rather than pick someone who represented San Francisco's sports establishment or big business to lead the bid, Lee and York wisely looked to an accomplished young rising star. Daniel had been very successful in recruiting and mobilizing an impressive combination of old money San Franciscans and more importantly, young, successful entrepreneurs from the tech and business community to raise and award almost $100 million in impactful grants through Tipping Point. Although Daniel had no experience in the world of sports, he was viewed as a person with the energy, connections and ambition needed to lead the bid effort.

Daniel has a very engaging way about him. When we met, he didn't try to come off as the smartest guy in the room; to the contrary, he was respectful, even deferential, in asking for my help and the help of others. We talked about the opportunity of hosting a Super Bowl, and how, if done right, it could lift up our community in ways nothing else could. It had the potential to be more than a game; it could be a real platform for good. That was his rationale for wanting to jump into this massive undertaking, and now he was recruiting a few people to help him figure out how we might get on the short list of cities to bid.

Daniel said my longtime experience with the San Francisco Giants and connections in the corporate community could really help if I was willing and available to join the bid committee. I immediately liked him and was flattered that he wanted me to be a part of it. I too felt an event like a Super Bowl really could make a significant social impact on the Bay Area in addition to an economic one, and if we did it right, it could be a model for future sporting events around the globe. The Super Bowl was the world's most-watched annual sporting event, but it could also make a huge positive difference locally if it was designed with purpose. I called him the very next day to say I was in.

That November 2012, the NFL shared the good news we would be one of the three cities permitted to bid for two available games. The San Francisco 49ers' promise of a gleaming new facility in Santa Clara had indeed turned our region's long Super Bowl drought into a realistic chance to be taken seriously as a host region. That meant we only had five months to assemble the bid, prepare our pitch and secure enough financial commitments to demonstrate to the NFL we ought to be given serious consideration. We had to formalize a plan, run like hell to pick up support and hope it would be good enough.

Once we won the bid in 2013, we transitioned from a bid committee into a host committee. We became the stewards of Super Bowl 50 on behalf of the entire San Francisco Bay Area region, and were responsible for turning the promises made in the bid into reality. The prestige of being at the center of the most watched annual sporting event in the world might be enough for some people to pursue this dream, but for our team and the stakeholders who would join us, we knew that hosting a Super Bowl in the Bay Area couldn't be just about football. We knew we had to host it the way the Bay Area residents would expect: proud, inclusive, authentic and giving, just like the Bay Area itself. This couldn't be a Super Bowl experience that could be plopped down in any city. It had to reflect our region's values, style and community spirit, or it would never connect with our residents.

In addition to hosting for the first time in 30 years, we were the first part of the country to really get the opportunity to host a Super Bowl as a region. The host city of San Francisco sat over 40 miles from the host venue of Levi's Stadium in Santa Clara. We had 99 other diverse and decidedly proud communities in between, with two big population hubs of San Jose and Oakland, plus the state's capitol of Sacramento with its own set of rabid football fans less than a two-hour drive away. How could we get them interested? How could we ever get them on the same page? Would they come to our events?

Our Host Committee team held the belief that if we could agree on the overall vision, be vigilant about protecting it and get others to buy in, we could make something very special happen in the place where we all lived and worked. It would require a high-touch and thoughtful approach by the entire team, but we believed it could reap huge rewards for everyone involved, especially our region.

Assembling an effective team that could attempt something like this called for people who had ability, experience and determination, and could put project objectives above their personal needs and desires. Experience has taught me that you aren't always going to get everything right at the start of a new venture, nor can you expect to assess every potential teammate accurately. But if you carefully recruit people who believe in the mission, it is possible to create a culture focused on purpose, problem solving and taking care of its people.

Everyone on our Host Committee knew we had just one opportunity to get this right, so to give ourselves the best advantage, we worked to align everything with our stated values as much as possible.

» Our organization's vision and values served as our litmus test in writing any plans and adding new members to our team.

» Our guiding principle ensured our small but intrepid group consistently planned and executed with our responsibility to the region never too far from our thoughts.

» Our faith in the importance of the organization's mission energized us to seek partners with equal passion and the resources necessary to help deliver an ambitious plan.

» Our trust in each other enabled us to tackle issues and other challenges proactively and as a team.

The Super Bowl is a yearly celebration of sport and entertainment, economic benefit and big business, and it is always an irresistible spectacle for hundreds of millions of people watching in person, online or on television. Host Committee CEO Keith Bruce often refers to it as the "most important four hours of the year." And our Host Committee would be right at the center of this annual perfect storm.

CHAPTER 1

"WE DO THINGS HERE WITH A TWINKLE IN OUR EYE"—OUR APPROACH TO BIDDING ON A SUPER BOWL

Pulling a Super Bowl bid together is not an exercise for the timid, and in our case, we had a few more hurdles than most.

We had no regional sports commission, state or municipal subsidies to tap like many other Super Bowl contender cities enjoy, and so we would have to raise every penny of support ourselves privately. And, because our only Bay Area hosting was Super Bowl XIX in 1985, there wasn't much useful historical information available.

By October 2012, we had assembled a small band of bid volunteers and assigned everyone the task of learning as much as possible about preparing a bid. Despite our collective experience, none of us knew exactly how to put such a bid together, how much money we needed to raise, or how we were going to convince various stakeholders from around the region to work together. Some of us talked to past host committee leaders from other cities whom were willing to share anecdotal information, while Danielle DeLancey took on the yeoman's work of compiling the answers for our bid response to the NFL's request for proposal.

For the region's bid for the 1985 Super Bowl, there were fewer expectations related to the bid. The League's criteria included:

» Minimum of 70,000 stadium seats

» Either a dome or history of temperatures during that time of year of not less than 50 degrees

» At least 40% of the number of hotel rooms needed for the teams, media and NFL sponsors must be within a 60-mile radius of the stadium.

For the 50th Super Bowl and ones in the preceding decade, the list of bid requirements was considerably longer, ranging from organizing and promoting of local fan experiences to securing practice facilities for the two teams to arranging transportation of NFL sponsors, ticket holders and the media to game week events, in addition to securing a suitable stadium and nearby hotel rooms.

We believed we had one significant thing that would improve our chances: Levi's Stadium. The new stadium being built in Santa Clara by the San Francisco 49ers promised to be a high-tech wonder, and would show beautifully on the big stage. Plus, we actually thought it was a positive that we didn't have much historical information to bog us down. But the truth was we just went for it because we didn't know any better.

DETERMINING THE ASK AND REFINING OUR PITCH

First, we had to figure out how to show the NFL we could actually pay for the thing.

In November 2012, bid committee member John Goldman joined Danielle and me in Daniel's offices at Tipping Point in San Francisco to sort out the best way to demonstrate our financial footing. We had to determine an overall pledge target, how much we should we ask individual companies to pledge and which companies to go after. There was no way to know at this point how much would be needed for our operations, but we knew we had to come to the table with something impressive. Depending upon the size of the region and the extent of the public activities for fans, previous host committees had reportedly spent between $30 and $70 million in hosting a Super Bowl.

What should our number be? I scribbled $25 million on the whiteboard in front of us and the group agreed that figure was a minimum. We believed a figure somewhere between $25 and $30 million would assure the NFL of the seriousness of our bid, but the reality of getting to that number seemed daunting. In my new role as chair of the development effort, I knew we only had a few months to make the ask.

We stared at the wall. What if we asked the biggest local companies for $2 million each? Experience told me that asking for $2 million rather than $1 million wouldn't necessarily be twice as hard. Getting 15 companies at $2 million each would, in theory, be easier than 30 companies at $1 million each. This was going to be hard anyway so we might as well give ourselves a fighting chance.

Next up, we tackled our legacy initiative. In our bid, we wanted to make a bold statement about what a Super Bowl could do for our region, so I put "25%" on the board. That meant we would devote a quarter out of every dollar we raised from corporate partnerships to go to nonprofits in our region. We looked around the table and agreed; we all wanted to be involved in something that had the potential to deliver real impact. It felt bold, but it also felt right.

With the region's leadership in philanthropy, we believed a significant community investment might make this project really resonate with local leaders.

Bay Area companies, particularly those in Silicon Valley, are known for doing bold, innovative things that often reverberate around the globe. If we could get the leadership of the right companies in the Bay Area to commit, realizing this vision of a substantial legacy fund could actually be possible.

As Johann Wolfgang von Goethe said: "Daring ideas are like chessmen moved forward: they may be beaten, but they may start a winning game."

We asked these leaders to help us redefine what a Super Bowl could mean to our region and the positive impact it could have, and without giving them any definitive commitment on what they could expect in return, these companies joined us at the table. We asked them to trust us and fortunately they did. Their belief in what we were attempting to do not only gave us the confidence that we had a chance, but also showed the NFL we had a formidable plan with the right support.

SETTING OURSELVES APART FROM THE COMPETITION

By February 2013, we were simultaneously working on the bid presentation and reaching out to potential partners. We had just three months until the presentation in front of the NFL team owners, so there was a lot of ground to cover in a small amount of time.

A Super Bowl bid presentation is essentially a sales pitch, so we approached the design of our bid just like anyone else going after new business: first, we identified the needs of the audience—the NFL owners and the League itself in this case—and then second, demonstrated how we would fulfill that need.

As best-selling author and marketing expert Seth Godin has said: "Don't find customers for your products, find products for your customers."[1]

Too often, salespeople focus on their product's attributes versus the needs of their customers in designing their pitches, and then don't understand why their pitch isn't connecting with their customer.

In our case, it wouldn't be enough to say that Bay Area is an ideal spot for a Super Bowl; that's only looking through the product lens. Lots of places have great weather, supportive stakeholders and could demonstrate the financial wherewithal. Plus, we believed the NFL owners would have more confidence in our competitors South Florida and Houston, who could both lean on their track record of experience. We were an interesting possibility, but with unknown capability.

We knew we had to appeal to the needs of the League and the owners, and show how we could meet them. Our bid committee had to demonstrate why the Bay Area would be a strong host region, and how we would be able to deliver on the NFL's requirement for a first-class fan experience that extended far beyond Game Day. And because we wanted the milestone 50th

---

1   Seth Godin: Seth Blog: "First, organize 1,000"

Super Bowl, we had to convince the owners we could deliver something that would reflect the significance of this moment in the League's history as well as help set a new bar.

So, what was our approach?

We started with a vision that spoke right to the heart of the 50th anniversary: we didn't want to just bring the Super Bowl to our region, we aspired to do it in a way that would set a new standard. Just as the NFL wanted to celebrate their past, we also knew this was an opportunity for them to celebrate the Big Game and make a statement about its future.

Our value proposition came down to two key focuses: what our region excelled in and how this Super Bowl could leave a legacy of social impact like none before. The San Francisco Bay Area is known for really good food, wine and innovation. All of this would have to be included in our story.

The San Francisco Bay Area is the confluence of global innovation and deep-seated cultural impact, a place where people constantly seek to make the impossible possible, and in the process, lead the world into new digital and social realities. Game-changing ideas are born here every day. We like to shake things up, so "redefining the Super Bowl" became our natural mantra. The Bay Area has a reputation of doing things with distinction, a bit differently than the others and all with a twinkle in our eye.

Connecting with Silicon Valley was an intriguing opportunity for the NFL. First, we had Levi's Stadium, a venue that promised to be the most technologically advanced NFL stadium in the country, situated in the heart of Silicon Valley. The NFL wanted to look to the future with Super Bowl 50, so what better place than here? Plus, there would be no wooden benches to worry about this time around.

Second, by the time we presented in May, we had secured initial commitments from some of the titans of the local tech community, companies that led the way in innovation and we imagined might be attractive to the NFL as future partners.

Finally, our true differentiator was our legacy initiative. It was the first time this level of financial commitment to support a host region's community had ever been included as a foundational element of a Super Bowl bid, and we wanted to show how it could bring the NFL's tagline "more than a game" to life in new and potentially profound ways.

The result: our bid came with all the prerequisites that would address every requirement, plus the bells and whistles we hoped would impress NFL owners. We did our research, engaged our advisory board and local leaders to help us build the best strategy, and made a pitch we hoped would stand out in that very dark room. Sure, we included everything about the Bay Area we believed made it great, but to give us the best chance of hitting the bull's eye, we needed to put ourselves in the shoes of our target audience and think about what would resonate best with them.

MAKING AN IMPRESSION

They say you only get one chance to make a good impression, so how we delivered our bid was just as important as what was in it. A bid response can be hundreds of pages long so they are traditionally put into some sort of big binder or presentation folder, and have varied in size, girth and decoration, from engraved steel to embossed leather-bound versions. Each year, contenders worked hard to put their most creative and distinctive foot forward, all while showcasing their regional flair.

With a key part of our pitch being how technologically-advanced a Bay Area Super Bowl would be, we believed our bid book had to be digital. One of our early partners, Apple, offered to provide us with free devices, so we thought it would be impressive to put our bid on a gold iPad mini—signaling our desire for the golden anniversary Super Bowl—and have it delivered in a solid white presentation box to each owner. Knowing that some of the owners might not be overly tech-savvy, we designed the presentation to automatically start once the box was opened: an elegant solution to reinforce our message. We thought we had a winning pitch in an impressive package.

A few weeks before the presentations were due, two significant problems arose. First, we learned that since Apple was not an "official" NFL sponsor—Microsoft had the computer category—so we couldn't put our bid materials on an Apple product. Second, we learned there was a $100 limit in value on any bid gift to NFL owners; at the time, the iPad minis had a retail value of about $800 each.

We didn't want to revert back to the overstuffed binder approach like every bid in the past, plus we were already in production with the iPad solution and the presentation boxes. After quickly considering the alternatives, Daniel and Danielle had an interesting potential solution. To comply, could we simply make the Apple logo not visible so there would be no discernible sponsor conflict? And could we also just ask each owner to return the iPad mini after viewing the presentation so there would be no gift value associated with our bid package? We would even include a paid return envelope to boot. We sent our request to our NFL contact and held our breath to see if this solution might work. The good news came in short order; we had received approval to proceed with our suggested solution. We sent off the golden minis, flew to present in Boston and returned home with the bid victory in our hands.

Post script: After thinking about asking each NFL owner to part with these beautifully engraved gold iPad minis, clearer heads at the League prevailed; the owners were allowed to keep them. No return envelope was needed.

KEY LESSONS

1. In fundraising, it can feel daunting going after what appears to be a big number. By setting a suggested minimum level of contribution per partner and limiting the total number of partners, we could be more focused in our approach. The result: a target number that felt more attainable.

2. How do you approach fundraising when you don't have any concrete benefits to provide in return? You focus on the value of being collectively involved. By focusing on our legacy initiative and how companies could actively contribute, we enabled prospective partners to see the long-term impact that could occur because of their involvement.

3. A sales pitch is most effective when it is built with a focus on the needs and aspirations of the key audience in mind.

As an outsider to the Super Bowl bid process, we knew we had to help the owners and the League see how the Bay Area would be the type of host region that could meet their various needs. To do so, we had to try to look through their eyes, not just through ours.

CHAPTER 2

"DOING GOD'S WORK"—CREATING OUR VISION AND VALUES

A t one of the first meetings our Host Committee CEO Keith Bruce and I had with a prospective partner, we were fired up at how engaged the company's CEO was throughout the meeting. The leader of a prominent Bay Area tech company, this CEO was asking a ton of questions and was very interested in our answers. The pitch was going well.

After about an hour, he sat back and was pensive for few moments as we anxiously waited for his response.

"Do you guys get a commission on this?"

Keith and I laughed, looked at each other and responded no.

"You are going to raise north of $30 million, give a quarter of it away to charity, and you aren't getting a commission?"

We both nodded.

"Wow...it's like you are doing God's work."

I smiled and thought to myself, well, not exactly. But what we were doing did feel somewhat like a crusade; none of us were doing this for the money. Each Host Committee staff member was making significantly less than they had at their previous jobs, plus we'd all be out of a job once it was all over. We each chose to get involved because we sensed it could be something great, something historic for our region and something we could all be proud of.

But maybe he was right. To accomplish all we needed to accomplish, it wasn't a bad idea to appeal to a higher calling. "Doing God's work" became a favorite saying of mine and, in turn, many of our team members, especially when talking with potential candidates. It described the enormity of the task ahead and also gave a peek into how our organization operated, with a lot of fun and our tongues firmly planted in our cheeks.

BUILDING OUR TEAM

Making something extraordinary happen usually begins with a big idea, and we thought we had that in spades. Redefine the Super Bowl? Yep, that's what we promised. So, when you have the audacity to say something like that, you have to build an organization capable of making it happen.

Our bid served as our organization's foundation, but there was no roadmap to show us how to fulfill it. We had about $30 million of value in pledges at this point, but no firm contracts yet signed. We had the beginnings of a fledging team, but no idea exactly what the organization should look like. We didn't have much, but we knew one very important thing: the type of organization we wanted our Host Committee to be.

By December 2013, we were a very small team of six. Keith Bruce, former president of Sportsmark and a veteran of many Olympics, World Cups and Super Bowls, was recruited to be the San Francisco Bay Area Super Bowl 50 Host Committee CEO.

Keith was the perfect guy to lead our team, with the presence and experience to take this massive project on. He not only had extensive global event experience, but he also knew many of the players at the NFL and major sponsors. When he asked if I would consider taking off my bid committee board hat to join the Host Committee and talked about the kind of people he was looking to hire, it all felt right to me. Keith and I spoke the same language and I knew we could make a strong team. He brought global event experience to the table and I knew the Bay Area sports and entertainment market as well as anyone. I agreed to jump back in, becoming employee #3, and assume the responsibility for marketing, partnerships and communications.

Danielle DeLancey was appointed our Chief of Staff. She knew the bid inside and out; no one knew it better. Nicole Carpenter came onboard to serve as Executive Assistant, Office Manager and all-round lifesaver. We grabbed big event strategists Rosie Spaulding and Stephanie Martin from the 34th America's Cup to lead our event operations and marketing communications functions, respectively. We had the beginnings of a great team.

This small group was encamped in a space loaned to us by Fortress Investment Group, our new temporary home after moving from our bid offices supplied by Boston Consulting Group. We were all sitting on top of each other in a few spare offices and our little company was beginning to take shape.

We all agreed that hosting a Super Bowl wasn't just about the football—it was about what a Super Bowl could do for our region. That's why this crew jumped onboard what felt like, at times, a runaway train. But with no dedicated human resources team or professional to take the lead, how could we recruit like-minded people, as well as stay away from the wrong people? We all had to get on the same page and fast. That meant developing our organization's vision and values even as we were developing the master plan.

A company's vision and values serve as the organizational guide that helps define the way a team functions, how the organization acts internally and externally, and keeps an organization focused while it churns out the work.

According to author Mark Lipton of *Guiding Growth: How Vision Keeps Companies on Course,* a clear compelling vision can make a marked positive impact on organizational performance and serve as a beacon for a company's direction.

"Visions need to challenge people, evoke a feeling that draws people towards wanting to be a part of something quite special. When a vision is framed as something that is achievable within a set amount of years, then it falls into the terrain of a strategic plan."[2]

We didn't have had a detailed roadmap yet, but we certainly had a moral compass to guide us down the path.

ARTICULATING OUR VISION

In the early days, we didn't have physical plans to show nor an understanding of exactly what we could offer partners in return for their financial and in-kind support; all we could do was try to sell the dream and ask them to trust us. To do so, we needed to be able to convey our vision in a way that would stick.

---

2   "Guiding Growth: How Vision Keeps Companies on Course," *HBS Working Knowledge,* February 2, 2003. Martha Lagace

An organizational vision not only helps to define the end game, but also helps people understand where they can plug in and contribute along the way.

Working with one of our early partners, Boston Consulting Group, Keith honed in on the five key points that would serve as our guiding vision for the Host Committee:

1. Produce a spectacular 50th anniversary Super Bowl, showcasing all the Bay Area has to offer, and celebrating the game's first half century while setting the stage for the next 50 years.

2. Create an innovative, technologically advanced experience that connects fans to Super Bowl 50, both here in the Bay Area and around the world.

3. Make a lasting impact in communities throughout our region by committing 25% of all corporate monies raised to high-performing Bay Area nonprofits, making Super Bowl 50 the most giving Super Bowl ever.

4. Deliver a Super Bowl experience that meets and exceeds expectations of the NFL, the fans, and the region—and makes the Bay Area a top contender for future Super Bowls.

5. Deliver a series of Super Bowl events that unites people like no other Bay Area sporting event has ever done before.

This vision was meant to inspire our work and remind us of our responsibility to the region, as well as help us build trust with potential partners. But would it connect?

We got our first bit of feedback as we continued working with Boston Consulting Group. As part of their partnership, BCG assigned two of staff members on a rotational basis to work with us as project managers. We were thrilled to see smart and motivated BCG senior managers and associates fight to work on our account. They told us they found our work not only exciting but also important. As they became more engaged in helping us to deliver the vision and regarded as members of our team, the value we all received was far greater than any of us originally anticipated.

Gallup research has found that active engagement of employees and customers around a mission is a strong predictor of business success.

"As employees move beyond the basics of employee engagement and view their contribution to the organization more broadly, they are more likely to stay, take proactive steps to create a safe environment, have higher productivity, and connect with customers to the benefit of the organization," according to Gallup.[3]

These early ah-ha moments with our new partners energized our senior leaders, and also showed our growing advisory board, local stakeholders and the NFL that our team did indeed have the ability to deliver.

SETTING OUR ORGANIZATIONAL VALUES

We all agreed developing our values in addition to our vision had to be a priority for our young company. With input from the team, our vice president of marketing and communications Stephanie Martin took on the task of drafting and building out

---

3   "Why Your Company Must be Mission-Driven," *Gallup*, March 6, 2014.

the organizational code that became one of the foundational building blocks of the Host Committee.

By the end of January 2014, we had a single statement that would become the guiding principle for our entire organization and our core values defined. Our guiding principle provided a simple way for us to communicate what we stood for, how we would treat each other and how we would approach our work every day.

HOST COMMITTEE GUIDING PRINCIPLE:

The Super Bowl 50 Host Committee is committed to creating a Super Bowl experience that is uniquely Bay Area, and celebrates our communities and people like no other event has done before.

Our Core Values:

» **Integrity:** *Approach every interaction with positive intent, and demonstrate respect for all our stakeholders. What we do is important, but how we do it is even more so*

» **Excellence:** *Realize our vision by delivering on the details and adding value every day*

» **Innovation:** *Raise the bar on every aspect of the Super Bowl by curating, creating and collaborating on novel ways to connect people and redefine the game*

» **Participation:** *Ensure every one of our experiences enables our community to actively participate, and create and share their own experiences*

» **Passion:** *Stoke the collective energy and civic pride of our staff, partners and volunteers, creating a true culture of fun and passion for our work*

» **Collaboration:** *Create an environment of mutual support and genuine interest that goes beyond Super Bowl 50, bringing together the region's diversity of insights, talents and perspectives to multiply our contributions and set an example for future events in the Bay Area*

» **Responsibility:** *Remain always focused on building, serving and protecting the legacy of our organization, being accountable for not only our decisions, actions and deliverables, but also responsible for our communities and resources*

Our guiding principle and our organization's values were not just words on a sheet of paper. They became the foundation of everything we did, from adding new members to the core team to recruiting volunteers to how we worked with all our partners and vendors. Making a decision that would affect the organization? The values served as the perfect check-off list. If it somehow violated our values, we didn't do it.

Throughout my career, I've seen firsthand that taking the time and effort in the beginning to stamp an organization's vision and values into your daily work can result in amazing and wonderful things.

I've seen how people look out for one another. They are moved to do things they didn't know they were capable of. They find reasons to help each other and opportunities to come together. They talk with and actively listen to one another. They are kind and respectful to each other. They celebrate each other's victories and accomplishments, big and small, along the way. And they don't need to be motivated or managed, just mobilized.

As Sheryl Sandberg said in her book *Lean In*: "Motivation

comes from working on things we care about. It also comes from working with people we care about."

The vision and values were resonating internally, but the real test would be taking them on the road to people who were not yet in the fold.

PUTTING VALUES AND VISION INTO ACTION - HOW WE HIRED

Hiring full-time staff to work any big event is a tall order and working for a host committee was no exception. Who would want to work harder than they ever had before on a project guaranteed to render them unemployed and for less money than they might earn elsewhere?

We needed a small, dedicated team with individuals who knew how to 1) make an event of this magnitude actually happen 2) meet the needs of our incredibly diverse region and 3) strike a delicate balance when items #1 and #2 were at odds. To help us find the right people, we turned to our values to guide us. If we were going to develop a culture of success, we would have to hire carefully, look for people who would buy into that culture and then unleash our team.

Embedding our values into our hiring process also helped us to meet my #1 criteria in hiring: no assholes. A graphic description, yes, but it got the point across to the staff. We would likely have to deal with some along the way, but we didn't want to make the task at hand any harder by having any of them on the inside.

I've come to believe that there are really only two kinds of people: the ones who solve problems and the ones who create more problems than they solve. We've all seen them or have worked with them. Both types can be highly educated, intelligent, attractive candidates who say all the right things. But the ones you must have on your team are the ones who are devoted to the mission and focus on problem solving. They are the ones you can rely on no matter what.

Problem solvers have the ability to be a part of a team or lead a team, depending upon the situation. They are calm under pressure, can always be counted on—particularly during the tough times that every company will go through—and will bring a positive, can-do attitude to work every day. They step up not only in the good times, but also especially during the challenging ones. And in my experience, they are also people who are fun to be around.

The *problem creators* can look attractive on paper, but for whatever reason, they tend to focus on the negative first—or worse—are dishonest or betray the trust of team. They get tangled up in interpersonal issues, give excuses on why they fell behind on deadlines or deliverables, or come to work with an unproductive attitudes and sense of entitlement. They can be a cancer to the entire organization, and for everyone's sake, should be avoided at all costs. In a mission-driven organization, most of them eventually get discovered and shown the door, but usually they don't understand why because they are too busy deflecting what was their responsibility. We didn't have time for this type of team member; we had to make every attempt to hire the right people on the first go.

Turns out having clear values made it easier to attract the right people, and quickly determine who would be in it for the right reasons. We met a lot of folks who were massive sports fans and thought it would be fun to work on a Super Bowl. What many don't understand is that when you work in sports—unless you have your name and number on the back of your shirt—you aren't watching the game, you are watching everything else. This work was going to be fun, but it was also going to be one of the hardest things people ever worked on. We needed people who, bluntly, could "get shit done." We used that phrase internally so often, we even had "GSD" printed on our coffee mugs.

Since we didn't have a human resources department, each of our senior leaders had to take the time to screen every prospective candidate for their teams. This wasn't necessarily ideal with our short-on-time situation, but it did enable those of us who developed the vision and values to be directly involved with the hiring of each new employee and have frank conversations with these potential hires.

Here are some of the things we shared with candidates so they could make an informed decision about wanting to join our family, and we could make informed decisions about their motivations:

» Why our organization was created and what we were responsible for. This was about way more than the game itself and we were looking for people who shared our common agenda. Big shots, prima donnas or slackers need not apply.

» What success could look like if we did this right. To get where we needed to go, we had to work together, course-correct along the way and trust one another in the process.

» Every team member had a specific role and every role was

vital to our success. We believed good ideas would come from every part of the organization, no matter your title or years of experience, so we needed people who were willing to step up and contribute.

» Self-starters only please. Regular check-ins would help keep us all on track, but staff wouldn't be micro-managed.

» The importance of looking out for each other and taking care of one another along the way.

» We would be transparent and will expect them to be the same.

» We didn't have it all figured out. Working together would be the only way we would figure it out.

» We would work hard and play hard. We had a serious job to do, but we would have some serious fun too. We were in the "fun business," remember?

» This work would result in something they would remember and could be proud of for the rest of their lives.

Setting realistic expectations with candidates at the onset was not only important to our organization; it is something every organization should prioritize as part of their hiring process.

Our prospective hires got to hear from the beginning how they would not only be actively involved, but also how they would have the opportunity to really make a difference. We found this expectation setting was particularly important with our Millennial hires. According to the Deloitte Millennial Survey 2016, "open communication, inclusiveness, and attention to the ambitions of Millennials really do foster loyalty...having a strong sense of purpose beyond financial success is also a key driver of loyalty."

Remarkably, the Super Bowl 50 Host Committee didn't lose one team member during the lifecycle of our work.

KEY LESSONS

1. Developing a vision and values may not feel like important first steps in building an organization, but they help define your internal culture, organizational identity and how you attract and retain employees. In our case, our vision and values were the underpinnings of our every action, and helped us to be consistent in how we approached our work and our stakeholders.

2. The importance of a vision is not only defining what an organization strives to achieve, but also enabling employees and partners alike to understand how they can contribute. To ensure everyone involved understood the importance, we consistently looked for ways to reinforce our vision and values throughout our two-year run-up to Super Bowl 50.

3. When a vision and organizational values are clearly and visibly stamped into an organization's make-up, the result can be a much more engaged workforce. Over time, culture builds around these values and deeper relationships grow, especially when the leaders walk the talk.

4. There are two types of employees: problem solvers and problem creators. Hire the former, avoid the latter. The trick is in ferreting out which one is which. You won't always get it right, but if you interview in alignment with your vision and values, you will have a better chance of identifying the problem creators at the outset.

5. During the hiring process, it's important to set realistic expectations of what the job entails with any prospective candidate without sugarcoating it because on average, one-third of new hires quit their job after just six months of employment.[4] By helping candidates to understand their role, how they can contribute and what is really expected of them from the onset, it can help identify those who should be on the team, and those who shouldn't.

---

4   "Onboarding 101 for Small Business HR" Bamboo HR, February 2014

CHAPTER 3

"L STANDS FOR LOSER"—BREAKING FROM TRADITION

Most football fans are well aware the NFL has the tradition of using Roman Numerals to commemorate the annual game. Beginning in 1971 with Super Bowl V, each following Super Bowl was referenced by its Roman Numerals, giving the game an epic and somewhat mythical distinction. Of course, it also annually sends many to Google to figure out what number, for example, Super Bowl XLVIII actually is.

Over time, the Roman Numerals literally became bigger than life, manifesting into oversized versions in each host city's fan village during Super Bowl Week, as well as printed and embroidered on thousands of different items for sale. They are the ultimate photo op, not to mention a merchandising bonanza. The League and the networks play them to the hilt every year.

Upon winning the bid for the 50th game back in 2013, we raised our hands up enthusiastically into the air, forming the Roman Numerals that would be ours with our fingers—an "L." You could almost hear the "wah wah wah" of a sad trombone as it dawned on some of us that our Super Bowl would be associated with the universal sign for "loser." Not a good look at all.

THE IMPORTANCE OF PERSPECTIVE AND PATIENCE

As our initial team came together in January 2014, the issue of the "L" became a hot topic. We decided to approach the NFL and share our concerns. Couldn't we use 50 instead, we argued, a number that felt more distinctive, heroic, more celebratory and, as our younger team members pointed out, wouldn't result in a hashtag that looked like a misspelling? #superbowll

We thought we had a valid point and hoped the League would agree, but League contacts were initially non-committal. At the time, we thought this issue wasn't a burning fire for the NFL as it was for us, but we later came to realize they had the same problem with the "L" that we had; they just needed to take a longer view.

This experience reminded us to be mindful of the objectives of our partners and see each situation from their perspective as well as ours.

In working with the NFL, it was important for us to remember two things. First, like any major global company, the NFL had a brand to protect and the Super Bowl is the biggest jewel in their crown, and second, when you are working with a large organization, persistence usually pays off.

Just as we were stewards for our region, League officials were the stewards of the Big Game. They had not only the right but also the obligation to consider how any decision would affect the legacy of this property. In this case, the NFL had to understand all the implications of deviating from the time-honored tradition of using Roman Numerals for Super Bowl 50 because those implications would be in play long after our Super Bowl was over. They had to take a measured and deliberate approach, and we had to respect that process.

And because the NFL was a large organization with much on their collective plates, we needed to be respectfully persistent with our requests. Our League contacts always listened when we had ideas, opportunities, or, in this case, real concerns. But to be heard, we had to remain patient and steadfast as our League counterparts were working on two Super Bowls ahead of ours. That meant two other host committees, in two other states, were vying for their time along with us.

When you approach any working relationship, it is easy to assume the worst when someone doesn't return your phone call promptly or a decision isn't made in a fashion you consider timely enough. Especially in today's world when emails get fired off over the transom regularly and can be very easily missed or misinterpreted on the other end. It's important to take a moment and place yourself in that person's shoes.

This experience also prompted another kind of action from our side. We wanted to build the relationship the right way with our partners at the NFL, and that called for getting some good old-fashioned face-time. I've always found that building successful relationships is easier once you've met in person. People tend to open up when you sit down together, and even better, share a meal or a drink, especially in the beginning stages of a working relationship.

Technology can help do amazing things, but there isn't yet an effective substitute for the power of human interaction.

In early 2014, we brought our small team to New York and Los Angeles a few times to meet our NFL counterparts and get the dialogue going. Those face-to-face interactions made a big difference, especially when presenting new ideas or programs.

Hashing it out in person made it easier to ask questions, build trust and get to the heart of any issues. And knowing how busy our counterparts were, we tried to be sensitive to everyone's time by picking our spots and coming well prepared.

When we returned home, we continued to build those key relationships by keeping the lines of communication open.

Whether it was short check-in meetings with all our leaders, one-on-ones or just keeping our NFL colleagues updated on our progress, we took a very proactive approach to communication to help ensure we understood everyone's perspectives. Nothing was ever assumed.

Ultimately, the trust we built between our staff and team members across multiple NFL departments was one of the keys to our collective success and helped us to navigate our two years together more effectively. We didn't always get a yes to our requests, but we always walked away from the proverbial table understanding each other's perspectives and jointly agreeing to a path forward.

DEFINING OUR IDENTITY – CREATING OUR NAME AND MARK

While we peppered the NFL for their thoughts on the switch of the L to 50, we tackled a less difficult issue but one that was just as important: our name. Originally, we were simply the SF Host Committee, a natural evolution from the SF Bid Committee. But being just "SF" wasn't representative of our entire region. We were Oakland, San Jose, Santa Clara, Santa Rosa, San Francisco and every city in between, a territory of over 7 million diverse people.

You might be thinking "it's just a name, who cares?" If you are asking that question, you aren't from the Bay Area. The fact is we are a mix of 101 very different communities, and that mash-up of different people, cultures and beliefs is what makes our part of the world so vibrant. We knew sticking with SF alone might instantly turn others in the region off.

But using just "Bay Area" alone wasn't going to cut it either. This point was made very clearly when we pulled together a small working group to discuss our approach to our name. Along with Keith, Stephanie and I, we invited our thought partners and "consiglieres" Nate Ballard and P.J. Johnston to give their input. Nate shared an example from a recent vacation trip to Puerto Vallarta, Mexico. When he and his friends were asked "where are you from?" they initially replied "the Bay Area." Upon receiving a blank stare, Nate filled in the blanks: "we're from San Francisco." Everyone nodded. "The Bay Area" didn't necessarily mean something to people outside of our region, plus, there is more than one Bay Area in the United States. We decided we must keep San Francisco in our title to be crystal-clear about our location, and became the San Francisco Bay Area Super Bowl L Host Committee. It was a mouthful, but we believed it was meaningful. With the name finalized, we could now focus on the tall order of designing our visual identity.

An organization's mark is the visual representation of its brand promise, so it has to be just right and our mark in particular would need to be especially hard working. It needed to communicate the spirit of the whole Bay Area, differentiate us from other host cities and reflect our region's values—classic, innovative, welcoming, and a little outside-of-the-box. Plus, we had a slew of requirements from the NFL, including our full name and the still-undetermined Super Bowl number. It would be one of our most important creative decisions.

Based on studies by neuroscientists, researchers have found logo design can make an emotional impact that influences both human behavior and decision-making[5].

From a skilled pool of local talent who wanted to work with us, we chose famed graphic artist Michael Schwab to create our visual identity. He understood we were translating our vision and values into a mark, and it would need to serve us for 2+ years. His previous work was spot-on with our aesthetic preferences and we were glad to see he was up for the challenge, just like our other team members.

After a few months of working together, Keith, Stephanie and I joined Michael in his studio in Marin County so he could present his latest thinking on several possible directions. In my experience, an organization's leadership team must make key creative decisions. They can't be successfully delegated. It really comes down to "I'll know it when I see it" and the buck must stop with the principals who created the original vision.

Because an organization's visual identity can have such impact on consumer decision-making, it's imperative to spend the time necessary to get it right. This requires active and thoughtful collaboration between the designers and your leadership team.

We collectively narrowed down the options, eliminating those that just didn't feel right, and finally turned our attention to the remaining one. We all stood behind Michael's desk, discussing what we liked and what we didn't, and finally what

5   Fitzsimons, Grainine et al, "Automatic Effects of Brand Exposure on Motivated Behavior: How Apple Makes You 'Think Different'", Journal of Consumer Research, Vo 35, June 2008, pp. 21-35.

moved us. Michael's assistant Carolyn slid the elements we liked around on the computer screen and then it happened. There was a collective silence in the studio as the pieces came together and there was no question we were looking at the right one. March 22, 2014 is a day we will never forget.

Two months of work, effort and focus had gotten us to this place. We felt we had landed on a mark that represented the richness of the Bay Area and was weighty enough to handle the heft of a 50th Super Bowl. The elements included:

» A "gold coin:" a circular shape to evoke a commemorative coin and celebrate this historic moment in football and in the Bay Area.

» A golden color palette: the logo's color reflected the golden anniversary Super Bowl being played in the Golden State.

» The sun's rays: a nod to the constant dawning of innovation that drives the people and businesses of the Bay Area.

» The Golden Gate Bridge: Michael chose a view of our region's iconic bridge at its most welcoming—as if it was extending its arms—to symbolize of the experience we desired for residents and visitors alike.

» A golden football: to represent the very best of the NFL and the Super Bowl, a celebration 50 years in the making.

Once it was ready, Keith and Stephanie flew to New York to present it personally to the NFL's brand team and we held our collective breaths as they sold the idea behind the mark. They walked the team through our thought process and the rationale for the elements, colors and inclusions. There were nodding heads and positive feedback, but the decision couldn't be that quick; there were others internally who needed to be consulted as well.

We waited for the verdict as anxiously as we did for our bid news. We tried to hold our emotions at bay in case the word from the NFL wasn't good but the mark was already making an emotional connection with our team.

Finally, we got the word; we would just need to do some minor adjustments to the font size, but the NFL did indeed like what we presented. No major changes necessary. I let out the breath that I felt like I had been holding for a few weeks and called Michael Schwab with the good news.

We now had a name and we had a mark that we loved. The only question left: could we use "50" instead of "L"?

PATIENCE IS A VIRTUE AND IT CAN BE DAMN HARD SOMETIMES

By May 2014, we were ready to host our very first press conference as the San Francisco Bay Area Super Bowl Host Committee. It had been almost a year since we won the right to host the 50th Super Bowl and we believed it was time to show what we had accomplished to date.

We targeted the first week of June and began to formulize our plan. We had our name, our new mark and some other good news to share: at that time, we had secured almost $40 million in cash and services. Good news indeed. We just needed to somehow be rid of that loser "L."

As the NFL was going through their decision-making process on the "L" versus "50," we started to get a bit punchy. At a San Francisco Hotel Council luncheon of 600 people where I was the keynote speaker, I shared my feigned disdain for the "L" in my usual tongue-in-cheek manner by making the loser sign with my fingers on my head from the podium. Our marketing communications head Stephanie Martin just about fell out of her chair. Later, she pulled me aside and threatened to put a horse's head in my bed if I did that again, a la the Godfather. She was of course kidding, but the point reminded me that everything we did was now under the microscope. I never made that dumb sign again. Well, in public anyway.

In May, we got the news that we (and especially Stephanie after the Hotel Council episode) had been hoping for: the NFL had approved the use of 50 and told us they were ready to release their official Super Bowl 50 logo as well. It took time, but we had all come to same decision. It was going to be 50 just as we had hoped.

Over two days in the first week of June, our announcement of the NFL and the Host Committee's use of the number 50 and the release of our official logos was widely covered, demonstrating to our whole team the real power of the NFL brand. I found it amazing that something like a logo announcement could make global news.

No surprise, there was a lot of discussion about the divergence for one year to Arabic Numbers. Some traditionalists asked how could we possibly do that? We, along with Commissioner Goodell, even received a very official looking complaint letter from an organization called the "Roman Numeral Society of America" for our poor treatment and disrespect of the "L." The organization may or may not have actually existed, but that letter was a keeper. You just can't make stuff like this up.

KEY LESSONS

1. It's human nature to place your own needs first, and not always easy to empathize or understand the place others are coming from. When partners come to the table willing to consider each other's perspectives, it usually is the basis for the best kind of relationships.

2. You can accelerate the building of a partnership through face-to-face interaction, especially when that meeting happens in the beginning of a relationship. Looking people in the eye can help you to better understand reactions you could never hear over the phone or see in email.

3. Ongoing, consistent and honest communication is the most important factor of any successful relationship, but it is not only about getting on the same page. It's vital to the success of any relationship to understand what is important to each stakeholder, listen to each other's points of view, and work together to arrive at solutions that can fulfill project goals.

4. With the impact logo design can have on stakeholders, an organizational mark should be meaningful down to the very last element. But to make a connective mark, the designer must be fully educated on all parts of your company's philosophy. A creative brief can only go so far. Just like other partners, our designer needed to hear directly from us to fully understand the human emotion behind our vision.

CHAPTER 4

"TURNING OVER ROCKS"—THE ART OF PARTNERSHIP SALES

I t was inevitable. We'd be all set up in a sleek conference room of some big tech company, ready to give our pitch: how the Bay Area would redefine the Super Bowl. It had such a nice ring to it and was a message we could deliver with passion and conviction. Niceties would be out of the way and we'd be primed to rattle off all the reasons why a company should partner with us. And then, before we could get our next breath, the CEO would invariably ask:

"So, what the heck is a host committee?"

It was a constant question during the 2+ years we worked to prepare for Super Bowl 50. What the heck were we and why the heck were we doing all of this? It was a fair question.

Inevitable question #1 would be followed by inevitable question #2. "Are you the NFL?

Sometimes it was easier to start with what we were not. No, we weren't the National Football League. We were our own not-for-profit company, with our own staff, and a board of directors and advisors. We were the ones working directly with the NFL on behalf of the Bay Area, but we didn't work for them. The NFL was, in effect, our customer.

Inevitable question #3. "Okay, then you must work for the 49ers?"

Not exactly. The San Francisco 49ers were the host club and key backers of our bid, but they had a very important task ahead of them in addition to running a football organization—completing and opening a new stadium in two year's time so it could host the team and, ultimately, our Super Bowl. We would explain how we worked closely with the 49er leadership, especially with CEO Jed York and President Al Guido, but we were a separate, standalone organization created solely to design and execute the vision for Super Bowl 50.

The reality? A host committee is really a start-up, but one with a definite beginning, middle and end. Similar to the Olympics model with a local organizing committee, a host committee is set up locally to fulfill the bid requirements as agreed upon by the host region—in our case, with commitments made by the cities of San Francisco, San Jose and Santa Clara—and it was up to us to figure out a way to deliver and pay for those requirements.

Host committees also serve as a liaison between the NFL and the host region, helping the NFL and their sponsors, broadcast partners and other stakeholders to find the right venues or vendors for their events, large and small, and charitable activities. For example, we served as the liaison between Bay Area communities and the NFL and its business partners to help to facilitate requests and get necessary approvals for communities wanting to celebrate Super Bowl locally. Essentially, our Host Committee was the organization that had agreed to get Super Bowl 50 planned, permitted, paid for and produced within a runway of roughly two years because there was no way that deadline of February 7, 2016 was moving.

Every time we met with a company, we educated them on not only what a host committee is and does, but also what our Host Committee would specifically do.

This was an important distinction; we weren't just here to knock items off the bid requirement list. We believed we didn't have a responsibility to any one stakeholder; we had a responsibility to all of them. They all were our customers as well, so to speak. Our pledge to everyone was that this Super Bowl would benefit our region like no other major sporting event had ever done before. With every Super Bowl, some fans remember how the game unfolded, some remember the halftime show, and some remember their favorite commercials. Our Host Committee believed a Super Bowl could be remembered for so much more. We believed this was not only our collective opportunity to shine as a region, but the Super Bowl could leave a legacy of impact that could be felt well after the last whistle was blown. That was why the heck we were doing all of this.

THE FIRST DOMINOES ARE THE MOST IMPORTANT

Raising the money necessary to support our operations was one of my key responsibilities. I called the process "turning over rocks." During the bid phase in 2013, we secured about $30 million in pledges, but we knew we needed much more than that, especially with 25% of our funds raised going to local charities. After our preliminary planning process, we determined we would need as much as $50 million or more. Lots more rocks would need to turned over.

With no municipal spigot to tap for money, Keith and I believed that having fewer, larger Bay Area–based corporate partners would be the best and quickest path towards powering our plan, as well as demonstrating we had the trust and financial backing of the region's major players.

Before we reached out to any local company, I asked my friend Bill Campbell for his advice on how we could make the most successful approach—his answer: make our "ask" simple. Since we wanted to approach some of the most accomplished and innovative companies in the Bay Area, he recommended boiling down our ask to one sheet of paper and going straight to the top.

In early 2013, Bill connected me with Nikesh Arora, who was the Chief Business Officer at Google at the time. Over a 15-minute phone call, we were able to sell Nikesh on the vision and our goal of bettering the Bay Area through this Super Bowl. He committed to a minimum $2 million pledge and said maybe they could do even more to help us. Our first pledge was now in hand and it was from Google. Simple seemed to be working.

Through subsequent calls and a meeting with Nikesh and Lorraine Twohill, their global marketing chief, Google came up with an impressive list of add-ons, such as allowing us to collaborate with Google's tech wizards to develop apps to help Super Bowl fans navigate Game Week, or using their fleet of energy-efficient buses for our transportation needs. They asked "would all of that be worth something to us?" Wow. I was stunned and grateful.

The next day, Bill called me with news that Tim Cook at Apple indicated they were also "in," and asked me to follow up with their General Counsel Bruce Sewell on the details. Bruce shared that Apple had two caveats—they weren't interested in any recognition and nor could we use the Apple brand outwardly—but they wanted to pledge a minimum of $2 million and give us an additional value-in-kind amount for Apple products to help us run the business of our Host Committee. What? And they just wanted to help without getting anything in return. What kind of company does that? The company whose tag line had once been "Think Different."

What immediately connected with the leadership at both Google and Apple was how this event had the real possibility of leaving a legacy for generations to come. The concept of directing 25% of their partnership funds to benefit the community made the opportunity feel more concrete. We knew we were onto something when two of the most respected companies in the Bay Area wanted to do more than we were asking. They became the first, and as it turned out, the most important "dominoes" to fall: being able to say that Google and Apple were "in" definitely perked up the ears of prospective partners.

Within a few months' time, we had our bid pledges up to almost $30 million from some of the region's leading companies: Apple, Boston Consulting Group, Dignity Healthcare, Gap, Google, HP, Intel, San Francisco Travel, Seagate, Value Act Capital, and Yahoo. Our financial footing for our bid presentation felt impressive.

There were still no guarantees we would get a Super Bowl, so all of this was "on the come" so to speak. Advisory board members like Rich Silverstein, principal at Goodby Silverstein & Partners, pitched in by assembling a creative team to help develop the initial "look and feel" for our bid presentation at a bare-bones materials-only cost we never could have afforded otherwise. Virgin America CEO David Cush chipped in free airfare credit with no expectation of anything in return. Other Bay Area leaders stepped forward as well. There was a spirit of "just let us know what we can do to help" from influential and extraordinary people from across the Bay Area. They enabled us put our best face forward in front of the NFL owners.

TURNING TO YOUR NETWORK

After the bid was awarded in 2013, we had to turn those raised hands into binding commitments, and then go out and get more of them. It was interesting to see how the dynamic changed once we became the official host. There was definite excitement about what was to come, but the sense of urgency was now gone. A Bay Area Super Bowl was now guaranteed, and the companies and donors who followed were not in a particular hurry to jump on board.

It is a good lesson in human nature and something to remember: when you are on the hunt and there is urgency in your ask, your position is actually much stronger than after you have bagged the prize.

In the middle of 2014, we turned our attention to a broader group of Bay Area companies who had the resources, energy and creativity that could help us meet our goals and contribute beyond the top-tier partnership level. We used the term "partnership" to include any business or interested party who could contribute something of exceptional value towards our stated goal. This definition was used to imply a much deeper relationship and level of responsibility than is reflected by the term "sponsorship." In a very real sense, they became true partners in the success of Super Bowl 50 because they brought not only their money and services, but also their ideas, influence and trust.

I knew the only way we could have a prayer in getting close to the $50M mark in cash and in-kind services was to have the "big guys" join with us and hopefully set an example for their like-minded peers. For companies who had the size, scale and reputation of being industry leaders, an investment in our effort "was just a rounding error," as Bill Campbell bluntly quipped to put it into the proper perspective.

We attempted to make our appeal directly to CEOs when possible because we were big on vision and short on time. We needed to connect with those at the top who could understand what we were trying to accomplish and how it could impact the region. With this moonshot approach, we had some hits, some misses and yes, a few backfires. The biggest challenge always is finding a pathway to the top. Getting to the CEO is always tough; there are full departments that deal with sponsorship pitches and CEOs normally never get involved. This is one of key values of having a deep "Rolodex" of relationships and a strong advisory group to help get to the C-Suite. Are any of our targets your personal friends? College classmates? Do you sit on some boards together? Maybe your kids are classmates? We were trying to turn over some boulders as well as rocks.

Never underestimate the power of your network. Whether it's getting pledges for a major sporting event, backing for your start-up or your foot in the door as you are starting out your career, it usually comes down to how effectively you care for your network.

Pay attention to your network, and treat those in it with respect; good people tend to want to help other good people. And remember, staying in touch is easier than ever in today's digital age, but there is no substitute for face-to-face or voice-to-voice connections. Email and social tools will never be as effective as real, sincere, warm, human contact.

It's also important to always be respectful to all prospects, no matter if they buy what you are selling or turn you down.

Sometimes customers aren't ready to buy yet and they can be approached at another time, or they move to a new company that is a better fit with what you have to offer. People always remember how you treat them, so a positive interaction can keep the door open for business down the line.

To secure the almost one hundred Host Committee partnerships of all sizes, I estimate it took well over 3000 sales calls to hit that number. Most of the calls took time and energy and didn't result in anything, but until you run down a lead and exhaust every path, you don't know if there is anything there. By consistently keeping prospective partners informed on our progress and abreast of new elements added to our plans, we were able to turn some early no's into future yeses. Sometimes timing is everything, so it's important to keep relationships friendly and respectful.

WHEN THEY COME TO YOU

Fortunately, we did have a few partners who came to us before we could even ask. We were blessed with not one but two law firms who raised their hands and said they would like to help us with Super Bowl 50. A host committee was like any start-up business; we needed typical legal support in forming the entity, and creation of by-laws, employment agreements, partnership contracts and much more.

One of the most respected people in San Francisco's legal community, Mary Murphy of Gibson Dunn, had pledged her firm's support in the early days of the bid and Mary herself agreed to join our advisory group. After we were awarded the game, she said they would continue to help on a pro-bono basis.

After we had secured the game, we received an unsolicited email from David Berger, a partner from Wilson, Sonsini, Goodrich & Rosati, a firm with an impeccable reputation as key advisors to companies in the Valley. I didn't know him, but Danielle and I decided to take a drive down to Palo Alto to meet with him. An engaging guy, David got what we were trying to do and said his firm would like to help too.

You learn to sharpen your antennae when you consider any offer of help, especially with something as visible and high profile as this project was shaping up to be. Was this something to pursue, or was this just someone else who wanted to "step in front of the parade?" We needed the right partners working with us—the problem solvers not problem creators.

As we drove back to San Francisco, I decided to once again call the guy who had become my most valuable but unofficial advisor, Bill Campbell, to check out this offer. Bill refused to join any committee, but wanted to continue to help us under the radar.

Bill didn't know David personally, but left me with a message in his typical gruff style that told me all I needed to know. "There are no dumb-dicks at Wilson Sonsini." Sounded like a solid endorsement to me.

But how would our friends at Gibson Dunn who had done so much for us already react to this? Would they be upset? Would they think we were ungrateful? Remarkably, neither Gibson Dunn nor Wilson Sonsini were asking us to pay for their services. They recognized how much legal support we would need with the enormity of our task, and like our other partners, believed in what we were doing. We could never have afforded to pay for this kind of support otherwise.

I set a meeting with our Gibson Dunn point person, shared how grateful we were for what they had done for us so far, and floated the idea of a partnership of sorts. I outlined on one page the idea: "Legal Partner of the San Francisco Bay Area Super Bowl 50 Host Committee" with a few suggested benefits they hadn't asked for. We would ask Gibson Dunn to handle half of the work and Wilson Sonsini to take on the other half, and they would work together to divide the work as they thought best. I hoped the gesture of a partnership would be received well and they would understand the logic of dividing up what was shaping up to be a mountain of legal work between two firms.

Then I shut up. My hope was this wouldn't backfire and we would wind up with nothing.

Fortunately, Gibson Dunn responded quickly and said the plan made sense to them and they would happily accept. Phew. Both firms became part of our brain trust. Firm founder Larry Sonsini agreed to join our advisory group along with Mary, while their assigned team members—David Berger, T.J. Graham, Lixian Hantover, Stewart McDowell and Danny Mandel—became an invaluable part of our team and really felt like part of our staff.

THE CARE AND FEEDING OF PARTNERS

Making the initial sale is only the beginning. In the spring of 2014, Keith and I—along with our new fierce go-getter of a partnership sales director Gina Beltrama—continued to focus on turning over even more rocks, our partnerships services team kicked into high gear. Making the sale was just the beginning; we not only had to create a hierarchy of benefits and assets—and determine how to allocate them appropriately to each partner—but also help partners developing activations begin their planning process. And most importantly, we wanted partners to feel engaged for the next two years, not just during Super Bowl Week.

While each partner bought into the overall vision and spirit of community, we knew that many of them would compare notes, especially as we introduced them to one another. Under the watchful eye of our senior director of partnership services Vicky Wijsman, and later ably assisted by Jesse Yeager, we took great pains to make sure every partner not only felt fairly treated based on what they were contributing, but also that they were fully maximizing their partnership. A rights delivery and client services superstar, Vicky was our grand architect, leading the creation of incredibly detailed plans and working with every major partner on how they would deliver their activation inside Super Bowl City or elsewhere in the region. Overseeing what we promised, what our partners promised to us and how these commitments were fulfilled required meticulous management, constant dialogue and having the instincts to know how to move things effectively forward, especially when there was conflict.

A considered approach to planning and communication is essential for any organization entering into contractual partnerships. It ensures expectations are set, milestones are met, partners feel informed and prepared, and everyone lives up to their promises.

Because the incubation period was two years from sale to execution in most cases and many corporations tend to focus on the very near-term, we set up regular in-person get-togethers to keep partners excited and engaged in 2014 and 2015. The goals of these partner events: highlight both milestones and progress to keep the troops excited, keep them informed so they were hopefully never surprised and let them know what was expected of them as they planned how to activate their partnership during Super Bowl Week.

These get-togethers also served as a great creative resource for our partners. By bringing them together, we created the opportunity for partners to get to know one another, share ideas and best practices, and learn from one another. For example, as we shared what a partner activation (the term used for a public fan exhibit) could look like, we called on those with extensive experience in creating activations to share their initial concepts and inspire those newer to the game.

Plus, we wanted to have a bit of fun. We all had a lot of work ahead of us, but we were in the "fun business," remember? Rather than hold these gatherings in some predictable, standard, ho-hum meeting space or conference room during regular business hours, we chose to produce high-energy presentations in spectacular settings that encouraged time to socialize. We focused on making our meetings informative, exciting and, most important, succinct and on-point. We found consistently demonstrating the vision and our values in action, and setting a clear standard for high quality across all work product resulted in partners who were inspired and in many cases, exceeded their original commitments.

To add to the atmosphere and fellowship, we followed these meetings with sumptuous meals accompanied by fine wine and provided access to world-class activities like Pebble Beach golf with a few former Super Bowl players who were friendly and approachable. By having Sonoma County Tourism, Pebble Beach Resorts and Napa Valley as destination partners, we could be very judicious with our Host Committee spending and, in turn, these partners got great exposure for their beautiful properties, food and wine. And for our other partners in attendance at these meetings, well, who could argue with going to places like Pebble Beach and Sonoma County?

It wasn't a surprise that attendance at our "partner summits" was always at capacity. We were establishing a reputation for doing things with a twinkle-in-our-eye, an appropriate balance of business and fun, and being focused on creating memorable experiences for our partners. To us, redefining how the Super Bowl experience meant every experience and for every stakeholder, not just during Super Bowl Week.

KEY LESSONS

1. You can't assume others will understand who you are and what your organization does. We constantly had to educate stakeholders over the course of our organization's entire existence why we were doing all of this. What may feel like saying the same thing over and over is actually just being consistent with your message. Audiences need to hear messages multiple times before they sink in.

2. When you are raising money, you have to look for signals and get a feel for when you are in the best position to make the close. Sometimes it comes down to urgency and the fear of missing out. In our case, during the bid phase, the reality of a short deadline and the question if we would win the bid or not was actually an advantage. Once the game was secured, there was still excitement but companies felt they could take their time with the game being two years away.

3. Tapping into our collective personal networks with a compelling message was vital to the success of our fundraising efforts. Especially when you have an accelerated timeframe for getting things done, your network can sometimes open doors that have been previously shut. Remember, networking is not just for sales people; continuously building and actively staying in touch with your network is one of the most important things everyone can do personally and professionally.

4. When you are turning over rocks, you not only need to turn over a lot of them, you really need to look at what is on the underside. Sometimes there is gold, sometimes it's just a few bugs that scurry out. Sharpen your antenna to find partners who are interested in more than just stepping in front of your parade.

5. To make any venture successful, you can't afford one unhappy partner. We found that by establishing trust, diligently dealing with any issues that arose and setting an early standard for the quality of the work product was paramount. The enthusiasm for what we were doing together became contagious, and in many cases, partners exceeded their original commitments.

CHAPTER 5

"CREATING THE SECRET SAUCE" — TELLING OUR STORY

A t Super Bowl XVLIII in New York, I ran into an old friend from my baseball days, ESPN's bombastic and lovable character, Chris Berman. ESPN had their broadcast set on Broadway and he offered to give our small Host Committee group a tour. As we walked, he told us he already had come up with one of his famous nicknames for Levi's Stadium once it opened: The Big Bell Bottom. We had a polite laugh but I had a feeling that certain companies at home might not be too pleased with that one. Fortunately, that name never stuck, but it was a good reminder of just how powerful a visual can be in expressing an idea and telling the story.

As we entered into the summer of 2014, we had just completed our first press conference and the pieces of the puzzle were beginning to fall into place. We had a vision and organizational values. We felt good about our hiring process and now had a dozen quality people working with us. We had a growing roster of partners of all sizes and investment levels. But I noticed our partnership close rate was beginning to slow. Our other team members were having similar experiences; initial conversations were happening but moving into working partnership mode was slower than hoped. The doors were still opening so why were we struggling to convert prospects or more quickly engage new partners?

In addition to the lack of urgency with our Super Bowl still a year and a half away, we knew we had a few issues to consider:

» First, there were still many people in the Bay Area who didn't even know we would be hosting the Super Bowl.

» Second, even if they were aware it was coming, most didn't know the extent of the public experience and how they could be a part of the celebration.

» Third, our message to redefine that experience was very broad, so even as we described our vision, some folks had trouble visualizing how it could possibly all come together.

Having not hosted a Super Bowl in thirty years, our region really didn't know what to expect. We knew we would have to constantly communicate our plans and educate residents about what the Super Bowl experience actually is, as well as what it could mean for the Bay Area. But to break through, we would need more than bold slogans. We would have to figure out to tell our story in a way that would stick.

CREATING SHARED VISION

It's one thing to explain what you do, but getting people to understand the "why" and "how" and what it means for them is a lot harder. We needed to demonstrate not only how Super Bowl 50 could be a boon for our region, but also how partners could actively help make that happen. Simply put, we had to create shared vision.

Achieving shared vision is a result of four things: defining what success will look like, articulating clearly and with passion what it will take to get there, enabling your partners to see how they can actively contribute to that success, and, ultimately, if you do it right, hearing them answer with a resounding "yes!" when asked "was this worth it?"

Our goal wasn't to convince someone to see something that wasn't real; it was about actively engaging partners so they could visualize the success through their own lens. To create that buy-in, you have to paint the picture with colors vivid enough to capture the imagination of others and enable them to see how they can be a part of that vision. In my experience, defining what success means has to be your organization's primary concern; you have to put a stake in the sand and proclaim where we are going and what that destination will look like once you get there.

I knew from experience how an impossible dream can actually come true if you can create shared vision. In 1996, I was part of the small but intrepid group who visualized, articulated and developed a new ballpark for the San Francisco Giants. It was during a tumultuous time in the San Francisco Giants history, when the team almost left the Bay Area not once but twice after years of dwindling attendance and we were playing in what many considered the worst ballpark in America—Candlestick Park. After having lost multiple elections on new ballpark concepts, we had yet another new plan, this time for the Giants to build their own privately financed ballpark on San Francisco's waterfront, and on a section of the waterfront that, at the time, no one dared visit at night. To give this dream a prayer of becoming reality, we needed a totally new approach. We had to paint a vivid picture and back it up with a believable plan that showed our partners at all levels how they would contribute in making it happen.

We created a portable tabletop scale model of the ballpark and brought it out to neighborhood groups and community meetings so people could visualize how it would look on the waterfront. The new park would be a magical place with all of the charm and intimacy of classic ball yards like Fenway Park and Wrigley Field, but designed with all of the modern conveniences of today; it would be as different from Candlestick Park as a ballpark could be. And to capture the very essence of the venue, we would conjure up the image of a batted baseball soaring over the ballpark walls and splashing right into San Francisco Bay.

Our task was to describe not only how it would look and feel, but also build faith in our organization's ability to deliver. We were upfront with our partners, ticket holders and investors; this would be difficult but if we all worked together and each did our part, it could happen. And, amazingly, it actually did. Since that time, the Giants have continued to fulfill on that promise, setting records for attendance and consecutive sellouts, and winning multiple world championships by delivering on that shared vision.

With Super Bowl 50, we were still 500 days away from actual playing of the game and plans were still coming together; there was no tabletop display to be had yet. How could we help people visualize the dream, let alone what success would look like, when there is no structure to show and plans were still in wet concrete?

SHAPING THE NARRATIVE

After a few more frustrating conversations with prospective partners in the spring of 2014, I locked myself in an office with Stephanie and Gina to try and get to the heart of the problem. We agreed: our sales materials were pretty but were dated and doing us no favors. They simply weren't enabling us to tell the story effectively enough.

Designed by outside sales consultants, we had one Power-Point deck that served as the base for all our partnership discussions. The information it contained was important, but it somehow wasn't resonating enough with prospectives, particularly as more detail on our plans became available. We had a conglomeration of facts, figures and images, but what we really needed was a more compelling way to capture their hearts and minds. Time to rip it all apart.

To create buy-in, we had to enable partners to develop an emotional connection with our plans and, in turn, confidence in our organization. In particular, with prospective partners, they had to see themselves as a key ingredient of our overall story.

According to Jennifer Aaker, a professor at Stanford Graduate School of Business, stories are 22 times more memorable than facts alone. "Your big idea needs a story. Stories fuel innovation. They hold the power to transform listeners; to take listeners on a journey that changes how they think, feel or act."[6]

At the end of our session, Gina, Stephanie and I had a new outline that would make the big vision easier to absorb and our story easier to tell. We would educate our potential partners on

---

6   Aaker, Jennifer "The Power of Stories to Fuel Innovation" Stanford Innovation and Entrepreneurship Certificate Program Course Overview.

not only what happens during Super Bowl Week, but also how their involvement could extend that experience to many more residents. We would share not only who the Host Committee was, but also why we as individuals were personally involved. We made our vision more concise and understandable, narrowing it down to three goals that showed how we were focused on creating a more inclusive, more celebratory and more philanthropic experience for our region.

» Most Giving: a legacy of local impact, unmatched by any previous Super Bowl, to help children and their families in low-income Bay Area communities

» Most Shared: compelling experiences that would go beyond the game, created and shared not only by us but fans of all ages

» Most Participation: opportunities for millions to participate beyond the game, whether in-person, online or at home

With our new outline in hand, we enlisted marketing expert Patty Hubbard and her incredibly talented team at marketing agency MKTG to help turn our words into a more dynamic deck of images and slides that also told our story more emotionally. The result: a presentation that clearly communicated what we were trying to get across and felt uniquely Bay Area.

As our final step, we invited one of our executive committee members Becky Saeger, a respected former Fortune 500 executive and veteran marketer who now advises growing companies, to listen to our newly honed pitch and give us a reality check. Becky had listened to thousands of pitches throughout her career and was an experienced customer of big event partnerships. We needed a knowledgeable buyer's honest opinion. Her response: our story now focused on the right things and it resonated. Good. We were ready to get back on the road.

It was still a sales deck so of course we made the partner benefits clearer, but what made the difference was weaving purpose into every part of the presentation and enabling our stakeholders to envision the pride they would feel when it was all said and done. Simply put, we emphasized what all this work was really about: the people in our community and not just football.

BRINGING OUR STORY TO LIFE—THE POWER OF VIDEO

Now we had our story better much defined, but we needed something to help us cover more ground. It was time to start engaging with other public and private partners, so we needed a vehicle that could create a more instantaneous connection to our work, and be used during public speeches and appearances as well as viewed on our website.

In the summer of 2014, we turned to our friends at Goodby Silverstein & Partners again and asked for their help in creating a vision video. Their creativity had helped us turn what could have been an ordinary bid presentation into something quite extraordinary on those iPad minis, so we knew they were more than up for the task.

Following a process similar to our mark creation, we pulled the Host Committee's key leaders together and honed in on the central messages the video had to portray. The following is the script developed by the Goodby team with our input. Set to music from a local band, these words were superimposed over the images of different Bay Area cities, local characters and innovations, the new Levi's Stadium and a few historic 49er moments, and lots and lots of Bay Area people.

We are the Bay Area. We do things a little differently. We've always been the disrupter. The provocateur. Enemies of the status quo.

We don't just embrace new ideas—we create them. We've changed how people think, love, and connect. Now we're re-imagining sports' biggest stage, the Super Bowl—as only the Bay Area could do it—with a brand-new stadium, celebrating our people and cultures across our regions.

And for the first time ever—25% of money raised goes to local nonprofits.

We're not just hosting a Super Bowl, we're redefining it

This short 90-second video became a real workhorse for us, not only in sales presentations but also to make our speeches more effective and, down the line, rally our volunteers.

Video allowed us to get to the heart of our vision in an engaging, emotional and easy-to-understand way that defined what this experience was really all about: our people.

Political scientist Robert E. Horn has studied the impact of visual language on improving human comprehension. "When words and visual elements are closely entwined, we create something new and we augment our communal intelligence... visual language has the potential for increasing 'human bandwidth'—the capacity to take in, comprehend, and more efficiently synthesize large amounts of new information."[7]

---

7   Horn, Robert "Visual Language and Converging Technologies in the Next 10-15 Years (and Beyond)," National Science Foundation Conference on Converging Technologies for Human Performance, 2001

For a lot of people, our vision video created an ah-ha moment. Suddenly, they understood what Super Bowl 50 could actually mean for our region. As I'd say whenever I presented, it did a far better job of telling our story in under a minute thirty seconds than I could do, waving my arms, through my normal 15-minute presentation.

PRESSURE-TESTING OUR MESSAGES

We were pleased with the initial response we were getting from our advisors and partners on our revamped deck and vision video, but would they fly with new audiences?

Sometimes when you only spend time talking with people who agree with you, you can miss what the market is telling you.

With such a large task at hand, we knew it was also important to gather insight, ideas and feedback from people who weren't involved in our day-to-day operations and could give us all-important gut checks along the way.

As change management expert Dr. John Kotter said: "Outsiders have the intuitive ability to continually view problems in fresh ways and to identify ineffective practices and traditions."

In addition to our Host Committee advisory group, one of our greatest resources was the Community Committee structure we put in place. Part-sounding boards, part-bell weathers, part-knowledge bearers, these committees met about once a quarter and focused on specific areas of our plans, such as communicating effectively to the region, embedding sustainability into our operations, and weaving arts and culture into our public experiences. We invited local experts from across the region including museum directors, leaders of local attractions, government agencies and seasoned professionals in a swath of fields to join these committees, with a total of few hundred people graciously giving us their time and expertise.

The first committee we convened was the Communications Committee, a group of marketing, media relations and social media leaders across multiple industries and representing all nine counties of the Bay Area. We couldn't have found a better group to give our new slide deck and video the smell test.

I walked through the slides and then unveiled our new video. Like I do with any sporting event, I paid more attention to the audience instead of the presentation on the screen. I saw nods and smiles, plus a few toes tapping. There were cheers at the familiar site of Joe Montana and Dwight Clark's famous play, "The Catch." Then the real test: what did they think? When most in the room asked for a copy to share, we knew we had a winner.

KEY LESSONS

1. By creating shared vision, partners not only better understand your goals but also can develop the desire to play an active part in achieving success. We found that by focusing on the impact Super Bowl 50 could have on our region and our people, partners felt inspired to participate, and understood how they could actively contribute.

2. Well-articulated stories not only help an audience better understand your goals, they also help bring to life what you are seeking to do. When you tell your story effectively, others will want be part of it and even help you tell it too.

Too many facts and figures can put people to sleep; a compelling story keeps them on the edge of their seat.

3. Inspirational images and video not only bring your story to life, they also help your audience better digest and share your message. Remember that prospective customers are looking for how your product or service can fulfill their needs, or impact them positively in some way.

4. When you only take insight and input from those within your organization, you can sometimes be guilty of drinking your own Kool-Aid. It's important to build a group of trusted advisors outside of your organization who aren't bashful in giving you those all-important reality checks.

CHAPTER 6

"BUILDING THE PLANE AS WE FLEW"– MAKING PLANS AND PLANNING FOR CHANGE

There is nothing more nerve-racking than launching something new, that is unless you happen to be doing that launch live.

We were a few minutes away from the unveiling of the 50 Fund, the nonprofit arm of the Host Committee that would help make our legacy initiative a reality. I ducked into the conference room to see if the show was ready.

The Host Committee conference room was in the center of our office space, with three walls of glass that allowed you to see anything going on inside. We had all our most important meetings in this room, so it was never a surprise to see team members trying to sneak a peek as they walked by. The day NFL Hall of Famer Ronnie Lott came through, it was practically a parade.

The conference room was now full of computers, screens and mobile phones, all lined up across the giant conference table that dominated the room. It could have easily been an ad for Apple. In one corner, Sarah Hawkins, our director of communications and resident social media maven, was furiously plugging away on her keyboard. In the other corner, vice president of community relations Jason Trimiew and our 50 Fund board chair Kamba Tshionyi were also heads down, typing away and then watching to see what would populate on the screens in front of them. It was a tense scene. The only person who seemed to be at ease was 6'5", 265 lbs. All-Pro Defensive End Justin Tuck of the Oakland Raiders who was happily texting away on his phone as the seconds counted down.

It was Giving Tuesday, December 2, 2014, and we were about to announce the official opening of the 50 Fund. We were ready to start accepting grant applications for the more than $2.5 million in grant money we were already set to give away.

People had heard of our initiative to give money to charity and our constant drumbeat of "25% of corporate money raised" made the message stick. But the 50 Fund itself was brand-new and the idea that we would give away grants a full year ahead of our Super Bowl was unheard of. So, I wondered, should we be launching something this important over a live Twitter chat? Should we be worried that no one might "show up"?

Social media was definitely not my forte, so I had no idea how this was going to work. Our marketing communications team was very comfortable with all things digital, so they asked me to remain calm and, more importantly, stay out of the way until it was time. That was easy because I trusted their instincts, but remaining calm really wasn't an issue. I had seen the meticulous planning that went into this event and saw how these plans would help us to meet our legacy goal.

CREATING THE PLAN

By June of 2014, our planning process was ready to go operational. We were planning for and rolling out physical events like our first press conference and now the launch of initiatives such as the 50 Fund and Business Connect, our supplier diversity program. It was gratifying that our first public programs were designed to directly benefit local residents and businesses.

Our senior team responsible for this complex planning was almost complete. Joining Keith, Rosie, Vicky, Danielle, Stephanie and me on the team were our financial advisor Ken Tamura from the Silicon Valley start-up world, our pro-bono legal advisors and experiential marketing specialist Chris Garrity, who was our Head of Innovation as well as resident DJ when we hosted events at our offices. We were later joined by Walt Dobrowolski, a veteran of multiple Olympic Games and other global events, who joined as SVP of Operations, and full-time head of finance John Amore, who had an impressive background with substantial Fortune 500 experience. To conserve our precious financial reserves, we only added team members when we were ready for them to hit the ground running and not just wait in the wings.

Loving a good acronym, we called ourselves the SLT—short for senior leadership team—and met every two weeks. With each member responsible for a key piece of the project and developing a corresponding plan of attack.

Planning is not sexy, but it's backbone of any business. It's been said that a goal without a plan is just a wish, and there was no way we wanted to walk away from this opportunity saying "I only wish we had..."

Like many companies, our planning process worked backwards:

» We knew what we had to deliver and the timeframe in which we had to plan and execute each element

» We had identified our target audiences and envisioned how we could meet their needs through our work

» We then determined what needed to be accomplished in order to get to our end goal

» Next, we identified and continuously refined the best courses of action as well as the resources necessary to get it all done

» We then built a project plan with milestones to move it all forward

» Finally, we continuously reviewed our joint calendar and plan every two weeks as we progressed to determine when we might need to pivot or adjust

Seems simple, and it is if you plan in a vacuum.

To a develop a plan that would enable us to meet our collective goals and timetable, team members had to take into account all possible interdependencies, which are the impacts their activities had on each other's work and, ultimately, on our stakeholders.

Co-authors of *Fast Strategy*, Yves Doz and Mikko Kosonen studied some of the largest global companies to understand how they could adjust to major shifts in the marketplace without negative impact to their business.

"One of our principal findings is that strategically agile companies have forged a new leadership model at the top...collaboration is characterized by frequency, intensity, informality, openness, and a focus on shared issues and the long term. Challenges to conventional thinking are encouraged—as are challenges and criticism from outside the ranks of the top team, so that the group's dynamics won't cut off its members from the rest of the company."[8]

Because our project was so complex, we created an environment where every senior member could express an opinion freely and share his or her concerns openly; there could be no "sacred cows." The best outcome was always meeting our objective, so when an issue was identified, we jointly decided on the best path forward and moved on. That way, we could course-correct as needed and keep our plans firmly centered on delivering for our stakeholders.

PLANNING FOR A LEGACY—THE MAKING OF THE 50 FUND

When we proclaimed that Super Bowl 50 would be the most giving Super Bowl ever, we had to determine not only how much money we would need to give away to earn that title, but also, how to ensure that money would have the greatest impact. We needed to be deliberate and thoughtful in our approach.

Process came first, with the establishment of a separate 501(c)(3) nonprofit organization—the 50 Fund—to help us give transparently and purposefully. We set up a separate Board of Directors so there would be no influence from the Host Committee fundraising side on which Bay Area nonprofits would receive the grants, and then recruited some of the region's top philanthropists and leaders in social responsibility to sit on this Board and help evaluate each application.

---

8   Doz, Yves & Mikko Kosonen "The New Deal at the Top" Harvard
     Business Review, June 2007

With an organization in place that could now accept dona-tions and gift them, we needed a plan that would turn those dol-lars into impact. When Jason first joined us in July 2014 to run our community relations team, and assemble and manage our foundation, he rightly commented that we could give away 100% of the money we raised and it still wouldn't be enough to solve every problem in our community. We needed to be targeted in our approach. If we wanted to make real impact, we couldn't afford to be a mile wide and an inch deep.

As a region known for its innovation, we honed in on funding nonprofits with innovative approaches and proven solutions to local challenges. We chose to focus on funding select organiza-tions that were making not only a dent in their mission today, but whose efforts were resulting in change that was lasting and scalable.

On Giving Tuesday, after six months of planning, we were ready to go live with our first two grant programs, a full year ahead of Super Bowl 50. It was important to us that we get mon-ey out the door as it came in so it could do the most good as soon as possible.

I had confidence our launch would be successful because we had built a plan focused on our target audience—local organiza-tions who were working to close the opportunity gap for chil-dren, youth and their families living in low-income Bay Area communities—and had worked together as a team to identify needs, resources and all interdependencies we needed to ad-dress along the way.

A gifted social impact leader with deep experience in commu-nity development, Jason designed our 50 Fund grant programs and campaigns to help high-performing Bay Area nonprofits to continue to tackle big, thorny issues, as well as scale their impact across our region and beyond. He worked closely with other members of the senior leadership team to determine all the support plans the 50 Fund needed, from operations and finance to marketing communications and event planning. He identified how to best communicate each available opportunity to the right target audience, the entire nonprofit community of the Bay Area. He conducted hundreds of hours of outreach to ensure every nonprofit who wanted to apply was aware of the opportunity and how to do so. He also adapted the launch plan to accommodate 49ers Anquan Boldin's schedule when we found out the 49ers would be practicing at the same time as our launch event.

During every step of the 50 Fund planning process, our team thought about how to best reach these nonprofits, how to talk with them effectively, and how to develop programs that would enable them to do even greater work and make more of a difference locally.

As Steve Jobs said: "You've got to start with the customer experience and work back toward the technology, not the other way around."

When the clock finally struck 1:00 P.M. on December 2, Giving Tuesday, I was ready to give it my best Twitter effort. Thankfully, others decided to do so too. The tweets started to flow as Jason and Kamba, another leader in the social impact space, began to share the news that our first 50 Fund grant program would provide up to five grants of $500,000 apiece. It was pretty impressive news to share, and it was only the beginning.

More chimed in when Justin and Anquan—who was able to tweet from 49ers headquarters before he had to take the practice field—shared why philanthropy was so important to both of them. Two great leaders on the field and two even greater men off it.

It was one of those days you dream about: months of planning came to life in a beautiful way. But to me, what was most impressive was the way our team came together to really think about how the 50 Fund could be our mission incarnate. It was a shared celebration that resulted in more than 150 nonprofits applying for our first wave of grants.

BREAKING DOWN SILOES

Senior leadership team members had to tackle a mountain of tasks with their respective teams and areas of responsibility, but one of their most important roles was ensuring that other departments were in the know about developments, progress made, problems needing to be solved and any other bumps in the road, all without wasting time.

It's easy to have tunnel vision, and focus on just accomplishing your own tasks and not the bigger picture, but when the left hand doesn't know what the right hand is doing, it can be catastrophic. Nothing can derail a plan quicker than a siloed organization.

It's actually similar to football. Each player has a role on every play, so when the ball is snapped, they not only all have to execute their part, but also be ready to assist others as the play develops. It can definitely be the difference between winning and losing.

In the early days, our staff did a lot of talking in our staff meetings and not enough listening. We were missing key opportunities and if it continued, we could have faced some serious challenges down the road. The workload was increasing, interactions were waning and you could see the energy slowly draining from our senior leadership team members. We had to restructure our meeting format quickly because each department had their pieces of the massive puzzle and eventually, they all had to fit together correctly. We couldn't afford any dropped balls.

What worked best for our organization was developing a master tracking system that allowed each department to see tasks and milestones at a glance and how we were making progress. Along with these milestones, we included the major interdependencies that would require departments to work together. Working with our partners from Boston Consulting Group, we devised a simple, visual system to map each major task and deadline so we could follow this work closely, do our best not to surprise one another and provide a teammate an assist when needed.

Breaking down siloes is essential to making any organization work effectively; it was the responsibility of every leader to encourage cross-departmental collaboration and make sure their people were talking with one another. Having a "boundaryless organization"—as former GE chief Jack Welch calls it—also promotes teamwork and is a much more fun way to work.

Our community relations team understood the importance of cross-departmental collaboration maybe better than anyone in our organization. Jason, along with his teammate, skilled community engagement strategist LaMecia Butler, was building the plans for not only our grant giving, but also for one of our most important initiatives, Business Connect. For Business Connect to succeed, it had to be engrained into the way we all did work every day.

A decade-old program of the NFL, Business Connect is designed to link diverse local businesses with contracting opportunities related to Super Bowl 50. We decided it was important to put our own "twinkle" on it to better reflect our region, so for the first time, LGBT and disabled veteran-owned businesses would be in the mix with minority and women-owned businesses. We wanted to be more inclusive with this important initiative, and with the NFL Events team now under the leadership of Senior Vice President Peter O'Reilly, they readily agreed.

The Business Connect program had the opportunity to be one of the real drivers of economic impact to Bay Area businesses. It was a chance for hundreds of caterers, specialty merchandise creators, event organizers, transportation providers, security specialists and other diverse local businesses to raise their hands to be considered as Super Bowl vendors. But it would only work if local businesses were aware of the opportunity, understood how to apply and had confidence the opportunity was real.

Jason and LaMecia set about their plans—identifying potential businesses, conducting outreach, educating business owners—like they did for the 50 Fund, but also focused on educating our Host Committee team and partners so they understood that diverse local hiring was a real commitment and the way the Host Committee did business. Our staff would be hiring many vendors and contractors so what better place to look for them than in our own Business Connect community.

One great example: when it came time to hire a company to

design, produce and package the Host Committee volunteer uniform kits. Once we had Dignity Health onboard as our official volunteer partner, our staff looked at the Business Connect database of companies to see if there might be any contenders to bid for the business. After a comprehensive review of several proposals, there was a clear winner: local minority-owned Bay Area business Way To Be. We selected them for not only their design, distribution and pricing, but also for their approach to sustainability. It was a significant six-figure contract that was a real boost for their business and opened new doors to opportunity, including winning the volunteer uniform business for Super Bowl LI in Houston the next year.

Featuring the color of the Golden Gate Bridge—international orange—the Host Committee volunteer uniform was designed to not only be highly visible to support out of town guests, but also to be something our volunteer team could be proud to wear. Each uniform contained recycled material, so with 5000+ uniforms produced, the volunteer team had effectively recycled more than 100,000 16-ounce water bottles. Fun fact calculated by our sustainability team: if you lined up those plastic bottles saved end to end, they would span the Golden Gate Bridge 7.3 times or the equivalent of removing 3 California households off the grid. Now that's what I call a win-win outcome for everyone.

KEY LESSONS

1. Successful organizations are best driven by interdepartmental dialogue and cooperation. By creating an environment that encouraged respectful discussion, we further fostered a strong organizational culture, and egos were

parked at the door. It wasn't about being the hero of the plan but instead satisfying the needs of the audience being served.

2. Nothing can derail a project quicker than siloed teams, especially in a small company. It wasn't always easy, but to be successful, we actively promoted the need for collaboration between work groups and willingly put our faith in each other's hands.

3. Just because you have a plan, it doesn't mean you stop course-correcting along the way. It is guaranteed something unforeseen is going to throw a monkey wrench your way. It's best to keep your plans in wet concrete versus set in stone so you can adjust along the way. For our team, this was particularly important to remember because in a very real way, we were building the plane as we flew it.

CHAPTER 7

"ONLY 70,000 PEOPLE GET TO GO TO THE GAME"—CREATING OPPORTUNITIES FOR PARTICIPATION

During the exploratory process for the bid, we were fortunate to have an impressive group of accomplished Bay Area people step forward with offers of help. One such person: former Secretary of State and National Security Advisor, and well-known football fan, Dr. Condoleezza Rice.

At one of our first gatherings of this group to review learnings from the 1985 Bay Area Super Bowl, we went around the room to introduce ourselves. Dr. Rice very matter-of-factly mentioned her previous jobs, asked us to call her "Condi" and shared that she was going to spend most of the night grading the papers from her Stanford class. That exchange immediately loosened us all up and we dove into the task at hand. Condi's big takeaway from Super Bowl XIX was quite profound: the Bay Area's last hosting had "no center of gravity." And she couldn't have been more right.

Aside from the game at Stanford Stadium and the hospitality tents for the ticket holders, there was nothing for local fans interested in the Super Bowl. There was no "there, there" in terms of a central place or venue where the community could gather together to celebrate. With Super Bowl 50, we wanted to somehow invite every interested resident of the Bay Area's 7,000,000+ population to be part of the celebration.

We all knew Super Bowl 50 should be a celebration for the many and not only the few, but the big question to tackle: where should that celebration be? Driving from Levi's Stadium in Santa Clara to San Francisco was 43 miles one way. Oakland was 38 miles away, in another direction. We couldn't shrink the physical distance between any of the region's major cities. The answer quickly became clear: there could be no "one" place.

Sure, there were the hardcore football fans who would drive (or fly) anywhere to be part of the madness, but we knew there would also be many residents would want to celebrate in their own communities or near where they lived. To create the inclusive Super Bowl experience we were after, there would need to be multiple centers of gravity.

CREATING THE REGIONAL CELEBRATION PLAN

With a modern-day Super Bowl, approximately 70,000 people can go to a Super Bowl game and thousands more go to the VIP parties and events that happen throughout Super Bowl Week. But what most people don't know is how the Super Bowl experience has stretched into a growing public celebration over the past two decades. Today, hundreds of thousands of people can directly participate in an ever-expanding number of local activities and events that come with hosting the Big Game. This isn't just one event for the few; Super Bowl Week now offers something for anyone interested, and we wanted to turn that hundreds of thousands number into millions.

To create a celebration plan that would encompass communities throughout the Bay Area, we knew from our collective past big event experience that plan would require two things: 1) educating Bay Area community leaders about what was possible and how they could participate and 2) putting strong public/private partnerships in place to successfully pull off each event.

We were very fortunate the tone of collaboration was set very early on when Mayor Ed Lee of San Francisco and Mayor Jamie Matthews of Santa Clara came together in 2013 to support the idea of a regional bid for a Super Bowl. That spirit grew over time once we won the right to host Super Bowl 50, and Mayor Sam Liccardo of San Jose and Mayor Libby Schaaf of Oakland joined our efforts. They all embraced the vision and wanted to create an environment that would actively invite Bay Area residents to the party. This was a very important foundation to work from.

The regional planning process began with the hubs of NFL activity. By 2014, we knew San Francisco and Santa Clara would be natural Super Bowl 50 gathering spots for visiting fans and residents with the game at Levi's Stadium in Santa Clara and the NFL Experience and Super Bowl City public experiences slated for downtown San Francisco.

The next step was getting more cities into the mix. As needs for venues arose over the next two years from the NFL and their vendors and sponsors, the Host Committee provided options from multiple cities to widen the reach. This approach led to use of sites throughout the Bay Area, such as Super Bowl Opening Night (formerly Super Bowl Media Day) going to SAP Center at San Jose and the Super Bowl Gospel Celebration going to the Paramount Theatre in Oakland.

While venue identification was underway, we also educated local community leaders about how they could participate in developing their own celebration. Bay Area cities are each incredibly different, so it was no surprise their approaches to engaging their residents in Super Bowl 50 were also individually unique.

For example, Oakland city officials and staff embraced the idea their city could be a driver of a lasting community legacy. The home to many of the nonprofits that were making a real difference locally and throughout the region, Oakland saw many of its own impacted early on by receiving significant 50 Fund grants. Jason and LaMecia from our community relations team worked with the City of Oakland to host some of our most successful community events in Oakland, including the kickoff of the Business Connect program at the Scottish Rite Center in 2014 and, reading events for The Re(a)d Zone, the Host Committee's signature early literacy initiative, throughout Super Bowl Week.

In the South Bay where the two Super Bowl teams would be staying, the cities of Santa Clara and San Jose were excited to welcome and entertain the out-of-state Super Bowl fans as well as the residents who wanted to be part of the Super Bowl experience. Rosie, Stephanie and Kyle Chank, our very talented Host Committee operations lead for the South Bay, worked with city officials and their staff, the two South Bay convention and visitors bureaus, and the San Jose Sports Authority to support the development of a very robust fan experience in each of their cities. Our staff worked closely with our Santa Clara and San Jose stakeholders for more than a year to support their planning efforts, whether it was sitting on their Super Bowl committees, getting approvals from the NFL, or supporting the creation of public celebrations such as helping to bring the Pro Football Hall of Fame's hugely popular Gridiron Glory exhibit to Santa Clara's Triton Museum, or promoting San Jose's daily outdoor fan experiences in their downtown parks.

As the host of the Big Game itself, Santa Clara was also the focus of significant logistical planning. Host Committee senior vice president of operations Walt Dobrowolski, director of transportation Kevin Solon and Kyle Chank all worked closely with the NFL, the 49ers and city departments in Santa Clara on the task of getting people in and out of the stadium efficiently and safely. It was more than a planning puzzle, it was also a major communications challenge; most of the 70,000 ticket holders for the Big Game would be going to Levi's Stadium for the first time.

Planning a major event requires significant time and resources, so our team focused not only on getting the dialogue going early but also learning the individual planning processes of our partners. Though we all had the same deadline, each partner had its own deliverables, internal milestones and processes that needed to be met, managed and fulfilled to bring each individual project to life.

Just as we had set up our own internal planning process, we had to learn and respectful of our public partners' individual planning processes to ensure our joint efforts could move forward as efficiently as possible.

Together, our objective was to create special experiences for all interested residents, so by surfacing our partners' individual processes and timelines, we were able to collectively identify where the Host Committee's participation in some form was helpful, necessary or critical to the overall plan success.

INVITING PARTNERS INTO THE PLANNING PROCESS

While our sales team continued to focus on turning over more rocks throughout 2014, our events, operations and marketing communications team members were out building the relationships necessary to create, run and promote more than a hundred of Super Bowl Week events. The breadth of the outreach we had to do would fill its own book, but there was one key that made it all work: deliberate communications.

Communicating clearly, consistently and constantly is essential to the success of any partnership. Communicating as deliberately as we did with our partners takes great effort and patience, but it can result in partnerships that are more collaborative and achieve greater results.

When you work in the "fun business," you understand better than anyone how important relationships are to getting work done. Whether it's applying for permits or partnering with law enforcement on guest safety and security, or in this case, working with communities across the region to create public fan experiences, it all comes down to a carefully-crafted network of relationships that is built to support each other.

For example, developing and delivering something as a complex as Super Bowl City required a myriad of committed partners, and hundreds of people at multiple local, state and federal agencies and other San Francisco stakeholders such as local businesses and neighborhood associations.

The Host Committee's free public fan village, Super Bowl City was to be located at the foot of Market Street during Super Bowl Week. In essence, we would be building a nine-day temporary theme park that could safely handle an estimated one million people in an area already inhabited and traversed by several million people every day. What on earth were we thinking? To some, it might seem easier to do something like this in a vacant lot way out in the middle of nowhere, but how would people get there? We were committed to delivering on our promise of "most participation," so a gathering place that was truly for everyone needed to be accessible by everyone—whether they walked, biked, took the ferry or arrived in a vehicle. It was an ambitious and, some might say, audacious plan.

Led by our major projects ringmaster, VP of event planning and operations Rosie Spaulding, the creation and delivery of Super Bowl City required not only vision but also an operational plan that covered every "what if." I can't adequately explain how much planning and how many details needed to be managed day in and out for more than a year, nor the breadth of the relationships needed. When you are designing and delivering something as large and complex as a public fan village that can welcome, serve and satisfy hundreds of thousands of people, you need someone in the lead who is guaranteed to knock it out of the park, and we had that in spades with Rosie.

Through regular updates, calls and meetings, we were able to address any concerns as they came, tackle potential issues immediately and arrive at creative solutions together. Touching base frequently with all the stakeholders who were working on Super Bowl City helped open the door to real dialogue, and encouraged all partners to share opinions, ask questions and contribute ideas readily.

The Partnering Initiative, a global program of the International Business Leaders Forum that is focused on proactively

promoting cross-sector partnership for sustainable development, identified good communication as the "heartbeat of all
effective partnering."

"Effective and continuous communication between partners
is fundamental to the partnership moving forward and to ensuring it achieves the hoped-for goals."[9]

Being deliberate in the way we communicated also helped to
build stronger relationships, in particular with the partners who
were critical to the execution of Super Bowl City during Super
Bowl Week.

TAKING THE CELEBRATION LOCAL

Big events and programs were now coming together in the region's more densely populated cities, but what about the rest? We
knew that residents would want to celebrate locally (it happened
with each Super Bowl), but we also knew that each of our par-
ticipating communities would want to celebrate differently (they
always did). How to do it was a much bigger mountain to climb.

One of the things we became sensitized to very early on was
the restriction on using the term "Super Bowl." As a registered
mark of the NFL, it carries great value and NFL sponsors pay
a great deal to be associated with it. The Host Committee was
granted restricted rights to use the term "San Francisco Bay
Area Super Bowl 50 Host Committee" and create a mark that
featured that term, but outside of that, we had to observe the
same restrictions as everyone else.

---

9   McManus, Sue and Ros Tennyson, "Talking the Walk: A Communication
     Manual for Partnership Practitioners" International Business Leaders
     Forum, 2008

We knew there was a very good chance someone in the local community would create a Super Bowl celebration sign, and no matter how innocently or well-intended it might be, it would have to come down. We wanted to be in the "yes business" instead of the "no business" and be able to say "here's what you can do" and not "here's what you can't." Enter the Super Communities program.

In early 2015, our marketing communications team designed a program-in-a-box approach that would give ideas, suggestions and guidelines to Bay Area communities wanting to celebrate the Super Bowl locally. Included with the box would be the opportunity to receive a city-specific Super Communities logo using the colors of their choice, for free. By providing guidelines and ideas, we wanted to not just invite communities to participate but rather proactively encourage them to do so.

Our pitch to the NFL focused on how these communities from all over the region could be included in a real way by enabling them to celebrate locally. To illustrate what we envisioned, we asked our superstar creative director Wes Wernimont to create a sample set of logos, banners and even t-shirt and water bottle designs using the words "Super Community," a football image and a place for the city's name. The visuals helped. The NFL team got what we were trying to do and not only approved the plan, but also allowed us to include our official Host Committee "gold coin" on banners as well. We were a bit stunned but elated to be able to offer communities the opportunity to use the official mark; each of these cities now could have the words "Super Bowl" printed on banners.

To introduce the program, we partnered with the City of Santa Clara, who were early adopters of the Super Communities program and one of its greatest champions, and hit the road in the spring of 2015, meeting with mayors, city managers and other city leaders to share the opportunity. We presented the program, walked through the guidelines and answered questions, and then asked these communities to contribute their own ideas.

By asking for a partner's input and ideas, you ask them to take the journey with you, and not just follow.

We could have easily just published the program, but we would have missed the mark completely; these people knew their communities better than we ever could. By asking for their input and enabling them to co-create, they not only helped improve the experience, they embraced the Super Community program in a way we believe wouldn't have happened otherwise.

According to marketing professor Venkat Ramaswamy, co-creation puts the human experience at the center of the enterprise's design. "Co-creation focuses on the experience of all stakeholders who would be involved in or affected by the new offering...the payoff of broad stakeholder co-creation is much greater personal engagement by all stakeholders."[10]

In the end, of the 101 Bay Area communities, 66 took up our offer and became Super Communities using our free kit to develop their own celebration. We were thrilled with the interest and response. Since my tiny community of Stinson Beach, a town of 486 on the Marin County coast, had no mayor or city manager to ask, I paid for a set of "Stinson Beach Super Community" banners myself and gave them to a local merchant, who promptly posted them along Highway One. For a few weeks at least, I was the unofficial Mayor of Stinson Beach.

---

10 Ramaswamy, Venkat "Building the Co-Creative Enterprise" Harvard Business Review, October 2010

DEVELOPING NEW WORKING GROUPS

No one can pull off a public event alone, especially one of the size of the Super Bowl. Just as each member of our team had individual pieces of the puzzle, so did hundreds of public and private partners across the region. Topics like traffic, transportation, crowds, safety and hundreds of other concerns have to be understood, discussed and tackled in advance. Potential impacts and inconveniences had to be identified, addressed and mitigated where possible. Community outreach has to happen early and often and the to-do list is long. The iceberg is much larger than anyone realizes.

Festivals, county fairs and gatherings of every kind and season are celebrated successfully—and safely—every year in the Bay Area. For each one of these gatherings large and small, there is a group of local public and private organizers who come together to figure out the logistics of public assembly, transportation, security and communications among other areas. This is the real work of the "fun business:" the art of keeping it fun and a bit unpredictable, and the science of ensuring everyone's safety.

For example, we knew from the beginning transportation was going to be one of our biggest opportunities and challenges. Fans, sponsors, League staff and the media needed to get to Super Bowl events around the region, while residents needed to go about their everyday lives as uninterrupted as possible. Many hundreds of thousands of people would be affected every day. To pull it off, we would need significant collaboration from multiple public and private partners.

In early 2014, our director of transportation Kevin Solon invited the 30+ different public and private transit agencies that serve the Bay Area to an introductory Super Bowl planning meeting with the Host Committee and our NFL counterparts. Kevin brought great operations and transportation proficiency to the table from his previous work on the Beijing Olympics, so he knew from past experience we had to accomplish two things with this meeting: engage these agencies in our vision and bring them together to build a master transportation plan for Super Bowl Week.

In working with multiple public and private partners—especially with those who have never worked together before—it's important to bring all parties together, face-to-face, in the beginning to establish roles, set expectations and understand each other's perspectives.

This level of inter-agency coordination had never been attempted in the region before, but having everyone in the room together helped set an early tenor of cooperation. Kevin asked each agency to share not only their focus and scope of service but also their transit expertise. Agencies were able to understand each other's roles, as well as our own role and that of the NFL. It was a successful first meeting that resulted in each agency committing to a joint planning process that would stretch right up to Super Bowl Week and beyond.

The work was painstaking and required a lot of heavy lifting and coordination to get all of the pieces of the puzzle to fit, but getting people to collaborate never was. Every member of this committee understood what a Super Bowl could mean for the Bay Area so they were committed to the effort of working together and creating the first regional transit plan of this nature. When we look back, we talk a lot about the legacy this Super Bowl created. To me, the inter-agency collaboration that brought fans, guests and residents together safely and efficiently during Super Bowl Week was one of the greatest results of Super Bowl 50 and, I hope, a working legacy that will live on.

KEY LESSONS

1. Every organization has its own processes and approach to project management and decision-making. By understanding the timelines and milestones that drove our partners' work, we were able to get ahead of their needs and remove any bottlenecks that our organization might be responsible for creating.

2. Clear and consistent communication is the key to any successful relationship. By opening channels of communication early, we found that partners not only kept each other better informed but also were also more willing to ask questions, problem-solve together and look for common ground. It wasn't always easy, but we saw huge returns on making partner communication a priority.

3. In creating programs and services for customers, don't forget these offerings are for them, not you, and their input and buy-in is vital. Whether it's surveys, focus groups or, in our case, in-person opportunities to get ideas and feedback, active stakeholder participation can not only help you design a better program, but also result in a more engaged and loyal customer.

4. For any partnership to work, it must be built on not only trust and shared vision, but also on clear expectations.

When working with multiple partners, it's important to establish clear expectations from the beginning, including how each partner will participate, the scope of their services, and the individual perspectives they bring to the project.

CHAPTER 8

"WHAT COULD POSSIBLY GO WRONG?"— LESSONS FROM THE FIELD

A two-year run-up meant two significant opportunities for our Host Committee to learn in real-time. First, we had the chance to talk with previous Host Committees who had already completed their Super Bowls, and second, we received behind-the-scenes tours to see Super Bowl operations in-person. It was the ultimate market research.

Because I was part of the initial bid group, I had the opportunity to see three consecutive Super Bowls up-close and increasingly more personal each year. My first included a power blackout mid-game in New Orleans. My second, a massive snow storm on the way out of New York. My third, a freak rainstorm in the middle of the Arizona desert. I was hoping our Super Bowl didn't mean locusts.

TURNING ON THE LIGHTS—NEW ORLEANS FEBRUARY 2013, SUPER BOWL XLVII

Our first experience came right in the middle of our bid preparation process and it was quite an introduction.

I've heard it said many times from Super Bowl-going veterans that New Orleans should be host every year and it's easy to see why; this was a town that could host a Super Bowl without appearing to break a sweat. You can walk just about anywhere you need to go, from the hotel to the French Quarter to the Superdome to the fan village to hundreds of restaurants, jazz clubs and bars. You can even walk down Bourbon Street in the middle of the night with a drink in your hand, or so I am told.

We didn't know until two weeks prior to the game that the 49ers would be a participant in Super Bowl XLVII, but we learned quickly what that meant: ticket madness. It seemed everyone in the Bay Area went into a frenzy trying to find Super Bowl tickets at the last minute, so of course, many assumed the local Super Bowl bid committee would be a likely source. Wrong. We had a handful of tickets provided to us by the 49ers, but barely enough to take care of our small traveling group. It was a small taste of what was to come later.

For anyone in the "fun business," dealing with tickets to the highest, hottest in-demand events like the Super Bowl or World Series can be a thankless task. As Arthur Schulze—the very wise longtime ticket manager for the New York and then San Francisco Giants—said long ago: "You never make friends in the ticket business, only enemies." What you learn quickly is everyone wants "good seats," they will pay for the tickets "only if they have to," and in the end, they aren't happy with what you did for them anyway. You just can't win. I made it my standard practice to respond "facing the field" to anyone who dared ask the seat location when seeking a ticket favor.

Our itinerary in New Orleans was simple as we were fully focused on building a successful bid response: meet with a few key

NFL staff members, look at all the Super Bowl venues that we'd have to address in our bid, and get time with New Orleans Host Committee to pick their brain. We were able to meet with NFL special event team leads Frank Supovitz, Dave Houghton and Mary Pat Augenthaler, and separately with New Orleans Host Committee CEO Steve Moore, all who had many Super Bowl productions under their belts and were incredibly gracious with their time despite the ensuing chaos around them.

We also got a dose of what happens when things go wrong. Shortly after the halftime show, the Superdome's stadium field lights suddenly went out. Scoreboards went black and no sound came from the public-address system. Players and officials milled around not quite sure what to do. I remember thinking about how the NFL, network and city officials must be in a collective sweat right now. Was it a terrorist attack? Were we in danger? What was going to happen? It was eerily similar to some vivid and terrifying memories from my past life.

It was a few minutes before Game 3 of the 1989 World Series on October 17, with the San Francisco Giants taking on the cross-town Oakland A's. Everything was coming together just as we had planned: Candlestick Park was fully staffed, decorated, teeming with activity and ready to go for the home opener. It had been 27 years since the last World Series game at Candlestick so the anticipation and nervous energy of the fans was palpable. The capacity crowd was just settling into their seats at 5:07 pm when suddenly the ballpark began to shake. I looked up at the scoreboard, which had already faded to black. The tower of field lights had just been warming up for the game and now they were out, swaying back and forth like metronomes. We didn't know it at the time, but a 6.9 magnitude earthquake had just hit the Bay Area.

As the San Francisco Giants vice president of business operations at the time, I saw firsthand how short the distance can be from the stressful excitement of overseeing preparations for the Giants' first World Series appearance in almost three decades to the helpless and sobering position of watching the ballpark shake, rattle and roll for 15 seconds, all without knowing what would happen next or what we could do about it. I can still feel that moment in my stomach when I think about it.

It was quickly determined by MLB Commissioner Fay Vincent with local officials that the game was not going to be played. They asked us to inform everyone to evacuate the building as soon as possible but there was one big problem: there was no way to inform them. There was no power and no backup power. No public-address system or scoreboards. The only mobile phones in 1989 were the size of cinderblocks and weighed about the same. Everything was down. All we could think to do was have the grounds crew run out and pull the bases off the field. When the fans saw that and the players walking off the field with their families in tow, they began to slowly make their way out of the ballpark. The emergency procedures for every major public assembly venue across the country were updated after that incident.

Everything felt scary and moving in slow motion, but people were counting on us to know exactly what to do. We kept our cool and our seat-of-the-pants decision making turned out to be solid. A stadium catastrophe was avoided by a few hours of remaining daylight, some quick thinking and a ton of luck. I had reoccurring nightmares about what it could have happened for years.

Now, three decades later, was I watching history repeat itself right in front of me? Thankfully no, it was nothing more than a power outage, and the New Orleans team and their local partners had planned for situations like this one. The backup power kicked in right away, and provided just enough juice to bring up the public-address system and a small amount of light inside. Thirty-four minutes later, the game resumed.

This experience further reinforced not only the necessity of planning and being able to think on your feet, but also the importance of a network of partners and other stakeholders who needed to work in concert with each other, especially when things go wrong.

Emergency and disaster planning for mega-events requires input from across public and private sectors, and months of planning for every possible "what if." This topic went to the very top of our checklist.

KNOWING WHEN TO PIVOT - NEW YORK / NEW JERSEY FEBRUARY 2014

The next year, we went to Super Bowl XLVIII with a similar agenda but a very different lens. We were now officially a host city so we were paying closer attention to the execution.

We were able to join an official Host City tour with the Arizona Host Committee, giving us an even greater view and insight into the intricacies of how a Super Bowl actually runs. One of the stops was the Handoff Ceremony, one of the annual rituals designed specifically to celebrate the handover from one Host Committee to the next. The Commissioner presides over the ceremony, which includes the handoff of a ceremonial football or helmet. Everyone smiles and shakes hands for the cameras.

It's a nice moment, but if you get close, you will see relief on the face of the outgoing CEO and almost hear the heartbeat of the incoming CEO beginning to beat faster.

Once your Super Bowl is over, one of your remaining tasks is to do a knowledge transfer with the incoming Host Committee. After the competition ends to get a Super Bowl, there is a camaraderie that develops amongst Host Committees; we are kindred spirits of sorts. Although the knowledge transfer is helpful, listening between the lines can be even more so.

A few weeks after the New York New Jersey Super Bowl, Danielle, Rosie and Stephanie flew to NYC to meet with their remaining Host Committee members, and Keith and I joined by the phone. I was driving in from my home in Stinson Beach to our office in San Francisco during the call. Our first point of discussion: how they executed the fan village and the NFL Experience outside in New York City in the dead of winter.

A gigantic pop-up football theme park, the NFL Experience provides an immersive experience for football fans of all ages. Players and alumni sign autographs and take photos with fans, and the media have a place to develop content around the sights, sounds and feel of the game. Aside from being popular with fans, the NFL Experience is the place where NFL sponsors and licensees can activate their products and sell their wares from pins to leather jackets and everything else in between. It has become one of the most tangible ways the NFL brings the excitement of the Big Game to life for fans and families. For a five-day show with lots of moving pieces, having good weather is not a major concern when you are indoors. But there was no indoor space big enough and available to host the NFL Experience in Manhattan. The Jacob Javits Convention Center was booked years in advance, and the trade show that had reserved the dates could not be moved.

Undaunted by the potential calamity of inclement weather and in what turned out to be a master stroke of showmanship, the NFL and the NY/NJ Host Committee decided to join forces and close 14 blocks of Broadway for a week to create "Super Bowl Boulevard." The pivot paid off. The weather cooperated and it was hailed a huge success, topped off by a giant toboggan slide running right through the middle of Broadway. One can only imagine the collective consternation and handwringing that must have been a part of that decision.

After congratulating the NY/NJ Host Committee on a job well done, we dove into our first question and were hit with a lot of information. Clearly, they needed to talk. The NY/NJ Host Committee may have had the toughest job of any host committee ever. Not only did they have to try and please two adjoining states, they also had the seemingly impossible task of holding most of the events that happen around a Super Bowl in New York City, outdoors, in February. I mean, what could go wrong?

I didn't count the number of f-bombs and other choice expletives that flew during that conversation, but there were plenty. As West Coasters, we thought maybe this was just how New Yorkers talked. They were ready to vent and weren't bashful in sharing their opinions or frustrations. Looking to break the tension, I mentioned I was driving across the Golden Gate Bridge and after hearing all of this, maybe I should just stop the car and jump off now. We all had a good laugh but I also thought: what the hell did we sign up for?

The laughter broke the spell. The NY/NJ team relaxed a bit and spoke about some of the good things, which were plenty.

I realized we probably had convened this call too quickly after their Big Game; they hadn't fully recovered from the aftermath yet. The sudden lack of adrenalin coursing through your veins after many months does funny things to you and we would learn that lesson soon enough.

What we also learned from that conversation was how important it was to have strong relationships, especially when you have to pivot or address an issue as a group of stakeholders.

Craig Runde of the Center for Conflict Dynamics at Eckerd College stresses the importance of promoting a culture that focuses on constructive conflict response because dealing with conflict is inevitable. "When conflict is managed well, it can lead to improvements in creativity and innovation, higher-quality decision-marking and improved implementation."[11]

Creating a 14-block outdoor fan village in February was no small feat, but by creating partnerships centered on problem solving, the NY/NJ Host Committee and the NFL were able to turn the potential challenge of hosting outdoor events in February into an opportunity.

MURPHY'S LAW ON WEATHER—PHOENIX FEBRUARY 2015

As we approached the one-year mark before Super Bowl 50, we had the opportunity to have a much larger delegation go to Phoenix for Super Bowl XLIX. This time, leaders from some of our corporate partners, key public officials from Santa Clara, San Jose and San Francisco and their public safety head honchos, and our staff leads all made the trip with their own checklists in hand.

11 Runde, Craig. "Conflict Competence in the Workplace" Wiley Periodicals. January 2014.

Many of the Game Week activities were held outdoors in Super Bowl Central, the Arizona Host Committee's fan village situated over about 6 blocks of downtown Phoenix near its convention center. Weather is typically great in the desert during winter months, but this Super Bowl Week saw several days of rain in the run-up to the game, dumping on much of the public celebration before turning sunny and perfect for Game Day. Ironically, the University of Phoenix Stadium had a retractable roof that was not needed on game day, but the downtown Phoenix could have used a retractable roof in the days prior.

But it all worked out, just like it had in New York/New Jersey the year prior. What you come to understand with a big event like a Super Bowl is that the fans will come despite the weather. They may have been expecting Arizona's normal sunshine, but no amount of rain or snow could dampen their spirits. Being able to show our sponsor partners the excited response from the fans to Super Bowl Central, even despite the weather, was extremely valuable and helped us close a few more partner deals while we were there.

What we realized once again is that relationships were going to make or break us. There would be no way we could accomplish all we were seeking to do without close working relationships that centered on trust.

As business management guru Stephen Covey said: "The ability to establish, extend and restore trust with all stakeholders—customers, business partners, investors and coworkers—is the key leadership competency of the new, global economy.[12]

In addition to fanning the staff out among the venues, we

12   Covey, Stephen "The Speed of Trust". Free Press, 2006

hosted our own partner event in downtown Phoenix and our first major media event with football writers—both artfully crafted by our talented director of hospitality Danaeya Johnson—and participated in our very own Handoff ceremony where we were on the receiving end.

The day before the game, Keith, Daniel and 49ers CEO Jed York joined their Arizona Host Committee counterparts and Commissioner Goodell on stage in the fan village and received their ceremonial footballs. Watching from the crowd with our partners, I could see the deep smiles on Keith, Daniel and Jed's faces, as well as on the faces of our partners reflecting back from the crowd; this was a truly proud moment. The event went off without a hitch. Fortunately, we had nixed the idea of Arizona throwing us the ceremonial ball. No way we wanted to chance a "San Francisco Drops the Ball" headline coming out of this event.

On the plane ride home, we collectively felt excited and energized. We got a deeper understanding of Super Bowl operations, had conversations with a variety of our stakeholders about what needed to get done, and even signed up a few more partners. With a week of 12 to 18-hour days and many miles of walking now complete, we thought that we had a good indication of what Super Bowl Week would have in store for us. Looking back on it now, I can see that we really had no idea at all what was to come.

KEY LESSONS

1. Seeking out the advice of those who have gone before you can prove to be invaluable. The experience might be different from yours, but there are always great nuggets of

information you can take away. Since we didn't have much historic information from our region's last hosting, having the opportunity to see Super Bowls in action as well as speak to previous host committees was an absolutely crucial part of our education.

2. Conflict can be incredibly taxing, but it can also push your organization to think outside of the box and get creative. The visibility that comes with putting on a Super Bowl puts organizational moves under intense scrutiny. To create a culture that focuses on problem solving and knowing when to pivot, leaders must set the tone and keep their emotions in check.

3. Relationships needed to be the hallmark of our work. Our senior leadership team understood that relationships of trust aren't built, they are earned, and require constant care and feeding. When you create relationships that are centered on mutual respect and trust, together you can create great things.

CHAPTER 9

"THE CLOCK RULES ALL"—TIME TO GET THE WORD OUT

W hen the date for your Super Bowl finally becomes official, the imaginary countdown clock begins to tick. Unlike a real estate development that proclaims *"Opening in Spring 2016,"* the Super Bowl clock counts down to an immoveable day.

In 2014, we thought it would be fun to display our countdown to the big day as part of our new office space at 825 Battery in San Francisco, the home building of Super Bowl 50's official broadcast partner, CBS-affiliate KPIX. Danielle went out and bought an inexpensive digital countdown clock and mounted it to the wall in our break room, a space that was open to the office and easy to view multiple times a day. I can remember one of the first times I looked at it while pouring a cup of coffee. "522 days, 5 hours, 58 seconds" it blinked away. Seemed harmless enough.

As days wore into months, the clock turned from an innocent novelty into a relentless reminder; it never slept, instead reporting the remaining days, hours, minutes and seconds every moment of the day. It was silent but constant and, in its own way, provided more motivation than any supervisors could and definitely a whole lot more stress. But it also reminded us that we had only one chance to get this all right, so we had to make the most of every minute of the day.

LOOKING AFTER YOUR STAKEHOLDERS

In the lead-up to Super Bowl XLIX in Arizona, we all had been working hard and the pace was definitely picking up. In one year, we had determined our name and logo, hosted our first press conference, opened our offices, launched the 50 Fund and the Business Connect program, built two websites, finally broke the 15-person mark on our staff and converted more than $40 million in Host Committee pledges to partnerships. We were officially drinking from the fire hose, but then we went to Super Bowl XLIX in Phoenix and saw it turn up another notch. It was exhilarating, fantastic and a week fueled by plenty of caffeine. There was so much to take in, and we tried to absorb as much as we possibly could.

The Super Bowl not only determines pro football's annual champion, it is also the time of year when the most business in and around sports gets accomplished, and the place where corporate America wines and dines their most important clients. Super Bowl Week is where key customer relationships are built and strengthened, where more sales are closed than any other time of the year, and where athletes, NFL alumni and celebrities can make big paydays without ever having to put on pads. Big business is always done in the lead-up to and at the Big Game.

A large part of this approach to business is the hosting of big bashes. There are more than 150 official Super Bowl parties and hundreds more happening around the periphery. Networks, sponsors, the Players Association, ticket brokers, merchandisers, game companies, the Pro Football Hall of Fame and the NFL itself all throw elaborate parties, VIP events and charitable fundraisers that stretch from the day well into the night. As a host committee, we were also responsible for hosting parties, such as the annual Media Party that welcomes thousands of members of the media from around the world, as well as creating a VIP "clubhouse" in Super Bowl City to thank our own partners for their help and support. Game Week parties are the places to be and be seen, and invitations to some of these exclusive events are as valuable and hard-to-come by as tickets to the game itself.

One of our other tasks as a host committee was to help the event planners behind these sought-after events do their advance work and accelerate the process of securing venues in the region. This meant identifying, cataloging and working to place holds on hundreds of venues throughout the Bay Area more than a full year before our Super Bowl. Hundreds of hours of meticulous scouting and securing prime event sites were done by our venue lead, event planner extraordinaire Sarah Louise Atkinson. Previously, this information was shared with the 300+ NFL staffers, vendors and sponsor partners who looked through big, thick binders as their take-home. Wanting to save everyone from a backache, we took the technology route to take advantage of the thorough legwork already done by Sarah Louise. Working with our smart and savvy website partners Channel 1 Media, we delivered to the NFL a simple password-protected database solution that the event planners could search based on any parameter from capacity and configuration to pricing and even venue photos, plus it alerted everyone each time a venue was booked.

Redefining the Super Bowl experience meant redefining it for everyone, not just the fans. We wouldn't have been doing our jobs if we left out any of our stakeholder groups.

Simplifying the approach to finding and booking venues had great ripple effects, making it easier on those looking for the right venue and a more efficient way for the local venue owners to showcase their offerings and rent their spaces. This simple tech solution saved all these stakeholders, including our own staff, a great deal of time.

CONNECTING WITH FANS (OR YOUR CUSTOMER)

Once your Handoff Ceremony comes to a completion—and you are now holding the ball—the previous host committee CEO turns with a smile that can only be described as maniacal and says "Congratulations, you are on the clock now." You smile, nod and take in what feels like at the time excitement of your region finally being the focus for the next year.

Then you hear it again. "Get ready, you are on the clock now," this time from an NFL staffer. Or twelve. Or from Commissioner Goodell. And no one warns you that being on the clock means the ticking not only gets louder but seems to go faster with every passing day.

When you are officially "on the clock," the spotlight is fully on your organization. The planning becomes more fast and furious. The to-do lists grow. The requests from partners and other stakeholders in the region become more specific, more frequent and definitely more urgent. And even though your organization has been planning for more than a full year, the public still won't feel the same crush of time as you do. To them, their Super Bowl is still a full year away.

In a region as busy as the San Francisco Bay Area and with so much ground to cover, we knew how important it would be to communicate early and often with residents. By February 2015, local football fans were aware that professional football's most important game was coming to Levi's Stadium in a year's time, but what about everyone else?

To reach our goal of being the "most participatory," we needed to let the public know what Super Bowl 50 would mean for all of them, not just football fans. Similar to our approach with our partners, we provided the public with information that was current, easy to access and digest, and was designed to be meaningful to them, not just to us.

One of our initial concepts was to own the number "50" and really highlight this milestone nature of this Super Bowl. Fifty was distinctive, something people could grab onto, and, hopefully, the region would feel proud to be the host of the 50th version of the Big Game. From the 50 Fund to our 50 Tour, we branded as much as we could with 50 so people could see the breadth of what we had to offer and how it was so much more than just four hours on a Sunday. Naturally, it made sense for us to kick-off this celebration of 50 at 50 weeks until game week, during the week of February 23, 2015.

Since we were already "on the clock," we decided to put the region on the clock as well, literally. Many big events have physical countdown clocks that fans can see in person, but that approach felt too static for us. We wanted something fans could engage with, not just look at. Our solution? A "human-powered" countdown clock. Our marketing communications team created an ingenious low budget but incredibly effective bit of promotional imagery that resided on the landing page of our Host Committee website. Managed and maintained by our unflappable Sarah Hawkins, this clock eventually ended up on television broadcasts and embedded in millions of pieces of digital communication.

To be on the clock, all you had to do was upload an image of yourself, your child, your dog or anyone (even my own bobble-head made the clock) holding a number between zero and nine directly to our website. When their day "came up," we would send them a nifty email letting them know they would be featured for the next 24 hours on the clock, as well as inviting them to email, post, tweet, share or yell out to their personal network to check out their day of being famous.

In their book *Made to Stick*, Chip and Dan Heath identified how concrete images help people to understand an idea more clearly. "Naturally sticky ideas are full of concrete images because our brains are wired to remember concrete data. In proverbs, abstract truths are often encoded in concrete language: 'A bird in hand is worth two in the bush'." [13]

The "human-powered countdown clock" fulfilled our three-headed monster mantra: it could be shared, it was participatory and it was giving (in a bizarre way). It was simple, irresistibly engaging and got us rolling earlier than expected, turning into a real head of steam for us with residents across the region.

---

13   Heath, Chip and Dan Heath "Made to Stick" Random House, 2007.

SHOWCASING YOUR VALUES

Launch week saw the clock kick into another mode for our staff. Being ever frugal, we didn't see the point of hosting an expensive press conference just to announce it was 50 weeks to the Super Bowl, plus we wanted to celebrate this moment in a way that was true to our organization.

With the opportunity for the human-powered countdown clock well communicated in advance to help us generate a wave of interest (and ensure we had some inventory come day one of the clock), we turned our efforts to what we called "surprise and delights." Super Bowl 50 was supposed to be fun so we wanted to start bringing the public in on the good times right away.

We kicked off 50 weeks until Super Bowl 50 with a celebratory countdown on February 23, 2015, working with our media partners to help generate some excitement and turn up the volume. We lit the sides of Levi's Stadium in Santa Clara and a beloved monument on San Francisco's Telegraph Hill called Coit Tower with projected golden 50s; it was our "bat call" out of the region to signal that, yes, Super Bowl 50 was indeed coming.

While part of our team worked on the lightings and starting up the countdown clock, other members of the team fanned out into the region, giving residents free surprise gift cards and gift certificates from our partners including Chevron, Gap and wineries around Sonoma County throughout the week. Teasing the locations on social media created intrigue and buzz, though the response to the freebies was also intriguing. We learned quite clearly that some folks are very suspect of free stuff!

Finally, we ended the week in a way that was authentic to whom we were—giving back to Bay Area charities and reinforcing

*to everyone what our mission really was. It was important to us
that our values were front and center in everything we did.*

According to communications expert Georgia Everse, it's important to connect your audience to the deeper meaning of an organization's vision when unveiling something new. "Messages that inspire are particularly important when you are sharing a significant accomplishment or introducing a new initiative that relates to your strategy."[14]

On the Friday of our 50th week until Super Bowl 50, we gave $2.5 million in grants to five organizations from the 50 Fund. Our "Game Changer" grants were $500,000 each, designed to support well-run nonprofits with effective programs that had the potential to scale and provide even greater impact. From more than 150 applications, our 50 Fund Board selected First Place for Youth, Fresh Lifelines for Youth, Juma Ventures, La Clinica de la Raza and Summer Search as recipients of our first round of Game Changers.

But we weren't finished there.

We also gave away our very first Playmaker grant, a $10,000 grant program from the 50 Fund that was targeted at community-based nonprofits doing work locally in their respective city or town. For the next 50 weeks, we planned to give away 50 grants—one per week—to an organization where $10,000 would make a real difference. But what I loved most about this program is that it also highlighted the herculean efforts of the people behind these nonprofits, the very people who were the difference makers.

---

14   Everse, Georgia "Eight Ways to Communicate Your Strategy More
      Effectively" Harvard Business Review, August 22, 2011

As Jason Trimiew had said early on, we needed to give smarter to make an impact that could last, so we developed a campaign around each of these 50 nonprofits. Partnering with social enterprise BAYCAT to bring each organization's story to life through video, we were able to support these nonprofits not only with funding but also with visual storytelling that could support their individual marketing efforts. These stories were inspiring, uplifting and, in some cases, downright tear-jerking, and for many of the recipients, this was the first professionally produced piece they'd ever had.

The Playmaker program took on a life of its own as the weeks started to count down. On "Playmaker Tuesday," you could find our community relations and marketing communications staff glued to their desks, ready to post, distribute and share these powerful stories with the world. The local media began to connect with these stories as well, and started to share them every week, on their broadcasts and online. These videos embodied everything we wanted the 50 Fund to stand for: creating impact and recognition for the nonprofits that do so much for our communities every day.

The work behind all our 50 Fund programs, from the outreach about the grants to reading hundreds of applications to the selection process to working with the nonprofits on their videos to the sharing of their selection and promoting their work, was in the thousands of hours. It was high-touch, hard and sometime grueling work by our dedicated 50 Fund Board and advisors, but it was time well spent. The result was the delivery of grant programs that connected some of the most deserving organizations in the Bay Area with funds to help them grow and serve more people.

Our 50-Week kickoff certainly took a ton of effort, planning and partnership to make it all happen, but we couldn't have been happier with the results. We kicked off the final push to our Super Bowl in the way we wanted—speaking directly to residents and in a way that showcased the values of our region. In a way, the weekly Playmaker grant announcements became the heartbeat of our organization, sharing a bit of good news every week.

Now, we had just 49 weeks to go, as the countdown clock reminded us every day.

KEY LESSONS

1. By thinking about ways we could constantly improve the experience for every stakeholder, we showed each of our partners how much we valued them and their time. Our venue-finder system and the ongoing support from our events operation team received rave reviews, and reminded us how we could make an impact through every stakeholder touch point by thinking smarter.

2. Initiatives can sometimes look great on paper but if they are hard to understand or communicate to our intended audience, the uptake will invariably be low. To generate excitement about Super Bowl 50 and signal the countdown was on, we created a concrete way for people to not only see the countdown but also participate in it and encourage others to do so as well. Sometimes the simplest ideas work the best.

3. To bring a mission-driven organization to life, it's important to walk the talk. For our organization, creating a real

community legacy from Super Bowl 50 was foundational to our efforts, so we looked for regular and specific ways to demonstrate that our commitment was genuine.

CHAPTER 10

"ADULT SUPERVISION"—TAKING THE MAGIC OF SUPER BOWL INTO THE COMMUNITY

T he whole point of a brainstorm is to generate ideas, see what sticks to the wall and then proceed with the best ones. Brainstorms work best when there is enough trust in the room for everyone to feel comfortable spit-balling ideas. After a year working together, there was plenty of spit flying in our departmental meetings.

One of our biggest brainstorms revolved around the Lombardi Trophies of the Bay Area. We realized early on that between our two Bay Area teams—the 49ers and the Raiders—there were a collective eight Lombardi Trophies. That was more Super Bowl wins than any other region in the country.

There is something special about a championship ceremony, that moment when the clock has finally ticked down and one team of victors finally arises. We've all seen that moment on television, and when it's our favorite team, we feel that moment of victory through and through. The champs return to the field where they have just conquered—now awash in champagne and confetti—and together hoist up that gleaming trophy, with bursting smiles and tears flowing. In that moment, all the effort, sweat and preparation poured into an entire season is richly rewarded.

The San Francisco Bay Area certainly has a lot to be proud of, so was there a way to capture a taste of that experience and share it with the region?

The idea to use the trophies in some way stayed on the back-burner until May of 2015 when we decided that a mobile tour would be the best way to share that spirit. Our Host Committee team believed a mobile tour could help us not only generate interest and excitement in Super Bowl 50, but with the trophies as the centerpiece, it would create more centers of gravity throughout the Bay Area. We were all onboard, except for the Raiders and 49ers, but that was only because we hadn't asked them yet. Now, it was time to find out if they agreed as well.

THE MAKING OF THE 50 TOUR

Making the 49er and Raider trophies this accessible to the public had never been done before, so we knew if we could pull it off, it would be something special for every guest. Time to make the big ask. I gave Raiders president Marc Badain a call while Keith reached out to president Al Guido at the 49ers. To our surprise, both teams thought it was a great idea and agreed to loan their individual trophies to us. We now had access to the 8 priceless and irreplaceable trophies for three months.

We pitched the idea of conducting a whistle-stop tour that would visit community fairs and public gatherings during the fall of 2015 in conjunction with football season, and enable the residents to get up close and personal with the trophies.

Our goal for the tour went beyond just a public experience; we believed it could tap into the innate pride of local fans and deliver a bit of the magic of the Super Bowl to each visitor.

Researchers have found people who strongly identify with a sports team have a greater sense of belonging and social connectedness, and feel emotional or nostalgic experiences when watching games. When your team wins, your faith and support is rewarded.

"When we look at motivation for following a sport team, group affiliation is one of the top ones. Identifying strongly with a salient local team where other fans are in the environment — that's a benefit to social-psychological well-being," says psychology professor Daniel Wann. [15]

With the okay from thse 49ers and Raiders, we selected the creative team at MKTG once again to help us figure out the details. As the plan grew and 50 Fund components were incorporated in to bring our mission to life, one of our corporate partners, Chevron, was excited enough to step forward and help us make the tour a reality. The 50 Tour was now on.

Rightfully so, the 8 trophies were the stars of the show. We turned an 18-wheeler semi into an impressive black and gold trophy truck that would unfold at each stop and allow fans to get up close enough to almost touch them. Surrounding the trophies were iconic images from each of those Super Bowls; Bill Walsh with his hands in the air, Joe Montana high-fiving his teammates, Marcus Allen soaring across the field, John Madden hoisted up on his teammates' shoulders.

15　Examining the potential causal relationship between sport team identification and psychological wellbeing. *Journal of Sport Behavior, 29,* 79-95.

Along with the trophy truck, we had the Chevron STEM Zone, an interactive space that demonstrated how science, technology, engineering and math (STEM) fuels innovation through the lens of football, plus a Kids Zone complete with a reading area for our Re(a)d Zone initiative and a NFL Play 60 Play On area where kids could run an obstacle course and catch footballs.

Each trophy was always given the white-glove treatment and protected with strict security guidelines to allay any concerns from the teams who entrusted them in our care. What was implied here was that we would not only take good care of them and treat them with real respect but, of course, return them in the condition we received them in. No pressure.

We put our director of marketing Michelle Villanueva in charge of the protecting the trophies. Triathlete and self-described "adrenaline junkie," Michelle had both the energy and the will necessary for this assignment. When on the road, she traveled with them, even surrounding her hotel bed with the trophies—each safely tucked in its own case—so she could keep one eye on them throughout the night. Another example of a team member doing whatever was necessary to make our promises a reality.

NOT ALL IDEAS ARE GOOD IDEAS

We had lots of good stuff to show at each stop. Now, how do we get the word out we're coming to town?

From my theme park days, I remembered an old-time Ringling Bros. Circus publicity trick employed when the show pulled into towns on the road. It was irresistible to the local media and always generated a ton of local buzz that the circus had arrived, which was good for ticket sales. One of the trucks carrying the elephants would invariably "break down" just short of delivering the performing pachyderms to the Big Top location in town. Animal trainers would solve the problem by hitching up the elephants to pull the truck the short distance to save the day. The circus PR department would do their part by notifying every TV, radio station and newspaper, which always resulted in an avalanche of free publicity about how the circus was saved by the elephants. Brilliant.

I pulled our marketing communication team together and presented my idea to get some publicity: one of the trophies would be mysteriously "stolen" from the tour truck to generate some media buzz as we pulled into town. We could then have the local police or sheriff save the day by "finding" the missing trophy. "If it could work for the circus, why not for us?" I reasoned.

Stephanie Martin, who was not only our point person for the tour but usually the voice of reason, patiently listened to my earnest but ridiculous suggestion and paused before calmly pointing out: "Um, Pat, if we did that, the tour would be immediately over."

Duh, of course it would. What would the 49ers and the Raiders think, the very people who were entrusting us with their crown jewels, if we pulled a stunt like this one? In this case, she was providing the adult supervision that was needed and quickly snuffed out my suggestion without calling or making me feel like a complete idiot.

All our senior leadership team members had to take turns wearing the adult-supervision hat. Brainstorming big ideas was fun and exciting, but we had to be realistic about what was possible within our time and budget constraints, as well as what might put us in hot water.

Being an adult also means treating fellow team members with respect always, because you never know when the next dumb idea will be yours.

TAPPING INTO STAR POWER

In September 2015, we prepared ourselves for our first public event for the 50 Tour: appearing as part of the NFL's kickoff celebration for the season in downtown San Francisco.

A two-day celebration marking the new season of professional football, our NFL Kickoff event was to include interactive exhibits, autograph signings, visits from the 49ers and Raiders cheerleaders and mascots, and a celebratory concert featuring multi-platinum signer Ellie Goulding and Grammy-winning band Train. It was a taste of what was to come during Super Bowl Week.

Normally, the NFL hosts NFL Kickoff in the city of the past year's Super Bowl Champion. But this was 50, so they did a simulcast from the actual game in New England and the celebration happening in San Francisco, highlighting the first 49 years and winking towards the future from the home of Super Bowl 50. It was great television and even greater exposure for the Bay Area. As a region that greatly benefits from tourism, getting some early network television exposure for the Bay Area five months ahead of our Super Bowl was huge, plus these early NFL activities helped to generate anticipation among local fans for Super Bowl Week.

It was also an event that wasn't on our radar at the beginning of the year. When the NFL events team asked for our assistance in early summer 2015 to bring NFL Kickoff to San Francisco, several members of our staff stepped up to make it happen. Though it added a big last minute task to our plate, we knew it would also be a great dress rehearsal for Super Bowl Week events and be a preview of sorts for Super Bowl City, which would be on the same site. It would also allow us to further build our relationships with Peter O'Reilly's events team and other NFL staffers in person.

Having the 50 Tour launch at NFL Kickoff was both helpful and challenging. This was the start of our three-month trophy tour and we didn't have the benefit of a paid advertising budget to support its promotion. NFL Kickoff would provide us with a built-in audience, but it came with a lot of other fun activities that the 50 Tour would have to compete with. To really take advantage of this golden opportunity, we needed a way to standout. We landed on staging a media event, and to cut through the clutter, invited two very important members of our Host Committee's Advisory Group and local football royalty to participate—Jim Plunkett and Steve Young.

In my experience, working with celebrities and famous athletes can be a mixed bag, but when you work with the right ones for your brand, they can provide a tremendous halo.

Celebrities and former athletes can perform at their best in front of thousands of spectators, but sometimes can freeze up and even appear to be standoffish in small gatherings; it's usually just because they are overwhelmed. Think about walking into a room full of 500 strangers who all know who you are, want to get close enough to have a conversation with you, and you don't know a single one of them. It can be a stressful and even intimidating experience for anyone.

With the benefit of perspective and, in recent years, media coaching, many former players have learned to enjoy the "meet and greet" opportunities that can be available to them. Being a congenial celebrity guest can be a lucrative new career. If you are a good enough player or coach, you can sometimes get away with being a jerk when you are in game-mode, but that doesn't fly when you take off the uniform, whether it's at the end of the day or for good. Fans and event organizers usually don't want to spend much time with current or former athletes who are perceived to have a bad attitude or think too highly of themselves.

We were lucky. The Bay Area is not only home to some of the best athletes who have ever stepped on a playing field, it's also home to some of the best people in the sport itself. Several Hall of Famers and past Super Bowl Champions from the 49ers and Raiders—such as Ronnie Lott, Marcus Allen, Jerry Rice, Dwight Clark and Joe Montana—still lived in the area, and they approached us to help.

For example, Steve Young stepped up to become a member of our Host Committee advisory board from the very beginning of the bid process. His football playing credentials aside, Steve is one of the most accomplished speakers I have ever seen. On one occasion, we asked him to be the featured guest at an important Host Committee fundraising event at the Fairmont Hotel in the

summer of 2015. We had handpicked a group of potential partnership prospects that were sitting on the fence and we needed
to somehow give them a gentle shove. With no notes and just a
quick briefing on what we were presenting, Steve gave an impressive and emotional speech on what we were doing and why it was
important. He conveyed not only what the Super Bowl meant to
him, but what it was going to mean to all of us. With no playbook
from us, he not only hit all the points we hoped he'd get across, he
hit multiple targets in our audience. After watching him work the
room, I believe Steve Young really could sell anything.

Needing the 50 Tour to break through during NFL Kickoff,
we asked Steve to join us at the podium once again and he willingly obliged. We also asked another one of our other favorite
Super Bowl Champions, Jim Plunkett, to join us as well.

A few months back, Jim and his Raider Hall of Fame receiv-
er Fred Biletnikoff—both Super Bowl MVPs—and their wives
not only agreed to come to our sponsor partner event in Pebble
Beach, but also stayed and hung out with our guests well into
the night. They could not be nicer or more approachable people, really no different than any of us other than the fact they
have hoisted a Lombardi Trophy in victory and wear Super Bowl
Championship rings. Playing in the NFL and making it to Super
Bowls was such a big part of their lives, Jim and Fred actually
loved re-living it all in the right setting. It made for a once-in-a-
lifetime experience for our partner companies: it's not often you
get to belly up to the bar with a couple of Super Bowl champions.

The 50 Tour press conference was remarkable to watch.
Members of the media and the fans alike were going gaga over
Steve and Jim, and rightfully so; they were expressive, polished

and genuine in their love for the Bay Area. It was remarkable to see one 49er and one Raider, standing side-by-side in front of trophies they had individually won, talk about how this tour could bring people together across the region. Moments like that reminded us of why we were doing all this work.

Then the floodgates opened. The 50 Tour was now officially kicked off and open to the fans, with eight gleaming trophies sparkling in the heart of San Francisco. Every selfie and photograph taken would not only be a keepsake for families who came, but would also be posted, tweeted and shared with the masses, helping us to meet our "Most Shared" objective.

Our volunteers were trained to take photographs for fans and how to answer the numerous questions that would be asked on the road. How much does each trophy weigh? Just 7 pounds. What is their height? 22 inches. Who made the trophies? Tiffany's. And some fans couldn't quite believe they were real. We loved to see their faces when we would verify they were indeed the real deal.

Every weekend from September to mid-November 2015—and some weekdays in between—the 50 Tour was on the road visiting another community and working its way around the Bay. Other former Super Bowl champion players joined us, providing free autographs, photos and, in many cases, giant hugs to the fans in attendance.

Raider Nation and the 49er Faithful came in force. We worried in the beginning that having the very proud fan bases of two very different teams together might prove to be tricky, but it was never the case. Fans didn't always want to take pictures of the other team's trophies, but there was always respect.

If you stood nearby, you could hear fans reminiscing about their own personal Super Bowl moments, such as three generations of 49er fans watching the game together as a family, or putting on their silver and black war paint every Sunday, together with fellow Raiders fans. One 49ers fan even shared how she was cheering so enthusiastically during Joe Montana's 92-yard Super Bowl XVI drive—the one that resulted in a touchdown pass to Earl Cooper—that her water broke. As she said, it was the beginning of the 49er dynasty and the beginning of her family.

Together with the Raiders, 49ers and our partner Chevron, we set out to celebrate Super Bowl 50 and give local fans a memory of a lifetime but when it was all said and done, we received a gift as well. Our team walked away with a greater understanding of the love Bay Area fans have for their teams and greater appreciation for the Bay Area's place in Super Bowl history.

KEY LESSONS

1. Not all ideas are good ones, but team members should feel comfortable in discussing and refining ideas openly and without judgment. By creating an environment where ideas are shared, disagreement is handled respectfully and constructive criticism is readily accepted will help move the project forward.

2. Working with celebrities can provide a great boost in exposure for your organization, plus the right celebrities can be a great pleasure to work with. It's important to go beyond name recognition and ensure a celebrity is a good fit for your brand. In our case, we chose to work with celebrities who were not only local sports heroes, but understood

our vision and appreciated what this moment meant for the fans.

3. For our staff, the 50 Tour gave us great validation that we understood what was important to our region's fans. Celebrating the Bay Area's place in Super Bowl history and the wins of the two teams was important, but enabling the fans to experience these wins in such a tangible way made all the difference.

CHAPTER 11

"GROWING THE FLOCK"—DEVELOPING BRAND AMBASSADORS

I t was less than 90 days before Game Week. Backstage, I looked over the notes one last time, took a breath and got ready to deliver my best Mike Krukow and Duane Kuiper-style welcome; my longtime SF Giants broadcaster friends were the absolute best at warming up a crowd. We had an audience of more than 1,500 people sitting out there in the darkness and their first impression of the Host Committee was going to be from me. I had to stick the landing.

Today, we were hosting our first volunteer orientation session in San Francisco's classic Masonic Auditorium, an indoor semicircular performance theater venue on Nob Hill that has hosted world-class headliners for over 60 years. It was a dramatic setting for musical performances, let alone our first gathering with our newly minted volunteer squad.

Like other major global events, the Host Committee volunteer program was crucial to our organization's ability to welcome the many hundreds of thousands of visitors and locals to the events around the Bay Area. Volunteers serve as key representatives for both the Super Bowl and for the host community itself, helping to welcome and assist visitors of all ages throughout Super Bowl Week as they navigate events and parties, as well as around the region. They are often the first person with which an out-of-town fan interacts, so they were important ambassadors.

The goal for the orientation was to educate the volunteers about the importance of their roles and do it in a way that would leave them feeling charged up and committed to being a strong part of the greater volunteer army. It was time to cue the show.

VOLUNTEER RECRUITMENT: CREATING THE CALLING

We started recruiting for volunteers in early summer of 2015. Based on past Super Bowls and our own plans, we knew we needed around 5,000 volunteers to help us spread out across the Bay Area and support fans at hotels, airports, transit hubs and major tourist destinations. Anticipating that there would be some attrition of volunteers as there is with most major events, we also set a target of identifying at least 7,000 qualified volunteers to ensure we could get to our goal.

Similar to the way we recruited our staff, we looked for volunteers who not only reflected the diversity and character of our region, but also got what we were trying to do. So instead of looking for people who just had a love of football, we looked for folks who were engaging and friendly, had a love for the Bay Area and wanted to share their enthusiasm with visitors. They would need to be knowledgeable about everything we were doing, and ready to welcome the world to our home.

As we promoted the opportunity to residents, local communities and interested employees of our partners to apply, our volunteer leadership team got ready to prepare for the onslaught.

How do you build an effective volunteer team? With lots of positive intention, attention to detail, and a strategic approach to selecting volunteers and getting them engaged.

"Volunteering, when channeled correctly, can be a highly valuable asset," according to community service leaders David Eisner, Robert Grimm, Shannon Maynard and Susannah Washburn. To identify a talented pool of volunteers, the team recommends, "...taking what we call a talent management approach—investing in the infrastructure to recruit, develop, place, recognize, and retain volunteer talent."[16]

Any given evenings or weekends over the summer and fall of 2015, you could find our enthusiastic volunteer staff of Alissa May, Ellie Kehoe, Heather Luna and veteran operations head honcho Walt Dobrowolski with their lead volunteer captains, winnowing down the online applicants through in-person screenings. With a dedicated group of volunteer screening specialists and other members of our staff pitching in, we had thousands of volunteer applicants come through our office doors, several hundred at a time. And like everything we did, we wanted to demonstrate from their first interaction with our team that this volunteer experience was important and would be an experience they would never forget.

Once the candidates came up the elevator at 825 Battery in San Francisco, the Host Committee's official offices, they would be immediately greeted by our giant Host Committee logo on the wall and a smiling face encouraging the taking of photos. First, they were whisked off to sign in and have their photos taken right near the infamous countdown clock in our break room.

16   Eisner, David et al "The New Volunteer Workforce", Stanford Social Innovation Review, Winter 2009

Volunteers loved the flashing red lights of the clock as much as our staff loved to avoid looking at it.

Finished with the sign-in process, they would be escorted into our giant conference room and be greeted by a Host Committee staff member. As any visitor to our offices at 825 Battery might tell you, our conference room was designed to impress and was something to behold. "Fun business," remember?

On two walls, we had a floor-to-ceiling photo of inside Levi's Stadium, so it felt like you were standing on the middle of the field and looking up into the stands around you. In the corners, we had a few set-ups of actual stadium seats, which you couldn't help but sit in. Cue the selfies. This was usually where I would be posted, seated at the conference table ready to entertain the applicants with my bon mots as they waited for the next station to be ready. I was always more popular when I wore my 2010 Giants World Series ring. Cue the second selfie.

Applicants would then spend time with a screening specialist where we got to know more about them and they got to know more about us. They learned about the types of roles they could fill and the pride we hoped they'd feel from helping to put on one of the biggest events the Bay Area has ever hosted. They also learned they would have to undergo an FBI background check. The Super Bowl is classified as a National Special Security Event by the Department of Homeland Security, so as part of our efforts to ensure the safety and security of volunteers and guests at Host Committee events, every one of our volunteers was required to undergo an FBI background check.

Finally, they would get their chance to be part of our website's Human-Powered Countdown Clock. Though anyone could submit his or her photos online, it was fun to offer the opportunity to be on the clock as part of the screening process. As they got ready to leave, we had a station of giant numbers that volunteers could hold while our staff snapped away. There were a lot of 4s and 8s for Derek Carr and Steve Young, respectively, while others choose their lucky number. No matter what number they chose, we got to hear their story, share a laugh or hear a favorite memory, and ultimately, get to know the person behind the number a bit more.

GETTING ORIENTED: MAKING VOLUNTEERS PART OF OUR TEAM

Those who made it through the screenings were asked to attend one of four major orientation events in late 2015 and early 2016 as the final step to becoming an official Super Bowl 50 Host Committee Volunteer. Our events team, with world-class event producer Kristi Calhoon in the lead on this project, prepared a show that was designed to not only educate but also fire up the troops.

The lights, sound and theatrics were ready, and the Host Committee staff were the stars, albeit reluctant ones. Most of us liked being behind the scenes and inside the iceberg a whole lot better than being center of the show. I was scheduled to open the first show and welcome the crowd. Fortunately, the volunteer team brought in two local stand-up comics to emcee the show and keep things moving.

I could hear our vision video belt out and knew my time was near. Kristi—looking official with her headset on and clipboard in hand—pointed at me, and I walked up the steps onto the stage and into the lights. As my eyes adjusted, I could see 1,500 people all up and out of their seats, screaming. I kinda felt like Mick Jagger for a fleeting moment. Butterflies were in my gut, but a calm took hold as I faced our first live volunteer audience. It was show time.

As the rest of the staff did their bits, I moved to a place where I could watch the whole audience and their reactions. I wanted to see their response to our vision and values, and what we needed them to do. Would they be as excited as we were? Would they get what we were doing? Would they understand that they were such an important part of putting on this 50th Super Bowl?

Over two hours, it was pretty amazing to watch. They stood, they cheered and they hugged. They roared with applause as Jerry Rice came on the video screen. They held five fingers on one hand and an "O" on the other up in the air, delivering our 50 with a flourish. They learned their own exclusive 50 fist-bump. They took selfies together and of each other, high-fiving and fist-bumping. Backstage, our staff's jitters turned into smiles and hugs as we saw what was happening. If I ever doubted how much people cared about Super Bowl 50 coming to the Bay Area, this crowd erased my doubts.

By enabling the people in the audience to understand how each of their volunteer roles would help realize the overall vision for Super Bowl 50, we saw them commit to joining us and accepting the responsibility of their roles right in front of our eyes.

In their book *Measuring the Impact of Volunteers*, Michael Fliess and his colleagues detail how volunteer engagement strategies succeed when they align the needs of both the organization and the volunteers. "When volunteers know their work is integral to the mission, they are more apt to feel truly part of the team, which builds a stronger commitment to your organization."[17]

Since we were close to the holidays, we also took this opportunity to ask the volunteers to also support the 50 Fund mission. We put out the opportunity for attendees to bring a toy or book with them, which would be then distributed to military families for the holidays. We hoped there would be some interest but didn't set our expectations too high. When I walked through the lobby right before the show was set to begin, I got the first clue about the enthusiasm and character of our recruits: the tables were overflowing with a mountain of toys and books. I don't think I could have been any prouder.

We followed that first orientation with three more and our "flock" grew to 5,500 folks. They were teachers, students, retirees and entire families from around the Bay Area. We had folks ranging from 14 to over 80 years old, and from all professions. It was an amazing mix of people whose energy and excitement matched the brightness of their Golden Gate Bridge–colored uniforms.

From that day until after Super Bowl 50, whenever I encountered one of our volunteers, we exchanged the 50 fist-bump with a smile; it was something special we all shared. Being a volunteer for Super Bowl 50 was a commitment, but it also was fun. For those who opened themselves up, it was an opportunity to welcome visitors to their region, meet new friends, share new experiences and create unforgettable memories.

---

17   Burych, Christine et al: *Measuring the Impact of Volunteers*, Energize, 2016

TAPPING INTO THE ENERGY OF YOUNG EMPLOYEES

As we ramped up our volunteer program, so did we ramp up our associate program. A group of enthusiastic young people commonly referred to as "interns" in most businesses, these team members joined us in the summer or part-time during the school year in the final run-up to Super Bowl 50. They were eager and smart, and made valuable contributions to our operations as they learned how a big event comes together.

Many were college or Masters students hoping to someday break into the business of sports. For some, this was their first foray into the inside of the iceberg; they learned firsthand what it takes to make the "fun business" happen. No matter your level, one day you might be working on a strategic plan and the next you are stuffing envelopes or holding a "lollipop," a hand-carried directional sign used to help direct guests at events or to their busses. Associates learned that no matter what the task was, it all laddered up to our overall objective. They were an engaged group of individuals who understood, just as our full-time staff members understood, that you did what needed to be done.

There were thousands of contributions made by our associates that helped make Super Bowl 50 a success, including notable ones where our associates took on a real leadership role:

» Elaine Cleland managing our media asset distribution

» Christopher Doherty designing our partnership asset matrix

» Maddy Kerr developing our online sustainability showcase

» Kathryn Petkevich leading our talent program

» Sheridan Spivey managing one of our Super Bowl City zones

» Kayla Wonderly serving as lead captain in our social media command center

Their collective contributions benefitted the project and the experience benefitted them as well.

What associates may have lacked in experience, they more than made up for with their go-getting attitudes and willingness to do almost anything to get the job done. For example, I was hopeful we could land a significant partnership from one of the mammoth global companies that in China, India or Japan are a household name. One such company was a powerhouse called Tencent, a dominant player in much of the world. One of their established brands, WeChat, was one of our targets. At the time, more people on the planet used WeChat than Facebook Messenger, What's App and Twitter combined. Surely, the investment would truly be a just rounding error for a company of their size.

A group of eager University of Oregon Warsaw Sports Management graduate students looking for a project took my idea on and turned it into a thoughtful, impressive and colorful presentation with our rationale, strategy and possible activation ideas. It was a great pitch, but could we get anyone at Tencent to listen?

For several weeks, none of my efforts in contacting the local office made any headway, so I called one of our first associates, Georgetown student Chris Tesoriero, into my office and offered him a mission: somehow get through to Tencent and deliver our presentation.

Chris was game for the assignment. "How do I do that"? was his first question. "Figure it out" was my answer. Chris came back to me after a few minutes and said "I don't have a car, but I found the location of their office in Palo Alto. I'm going to take the train down and walk to their office with the presentation. Train fare is only about $5."

I dug into my pocket, gave Chris a $20 bill and wished him well. "Don't come back until you break through," I said, with a wink. I wanted to see what he could do.

Chris not only got our presentation to the right person, but that person contacted me a week later to tell me how impressed he was with Chris himself. We ultimately didn't make the sale, but I'll never forget Chris' resourcefulness in breaking down the figurative door, and I bet he won't either.

When I look back on what the Super Bowl 50 Host Committee crew accomplished, I reflect on the complete effort, and the combination of how youth and experience worked so well together to get the job done. Adding youth to our mix gave us the benefit of some great thinking and smart approaches to problem solving.

According to leadership and ethics professor Katherine Phillips, "If you want to build teams or organizations capable of innovating, you need diversity. Diversity enhances creativity. It encourages the search for novel information and perspectives, leading to better decision making and problem solving."[18]

After the Super Bowl ended, those new to the "fun business" fretted about leaving the Host Committee and our daily experience together. For them, it felt final. But for those of us with previous big event experience, we knew the memories of how we all came together and made this experience happen would keep us connected forever. We were like members of a family.

---

18   Phillips, Katherine "How Diversity Makes Us Smarter" *Scientific American*, October, 2014

KEY LESSONS

1. Whether for an event like the Super Bowl, a nonprofit organization or a company, creating a high-impact volunteer program requires substantial planning, clear alignment back to your organization's mission and goals, and a systemic approach to attracting and engaging volunteers. Not all volunteers are created the same, so we selected volunteers the way we hired employees: making sure they were in it for the right reasons.

2. Don't forget your employees can be your most powerful brand ambassadors. Just as you educate consumers about your organization's offerings, it's important for your employees to be fully educated as well. The more connected they feel to the organization and its mission, the more likely they are to live the brand externally as well as internally.

3. The best ideas are not confined to those who have the most experience. Adding a small cadre of the next generation of leaders to the mix can make your organization stronger. When you pull a group of people together with different backgrounds, experience and expertise, the result is a diversity of thought that can help organizations better innovate and problem solve.

CHAPTER 12

"DRINKING FROM THE FIRE HOSE" — WHEN LEADERS ARE MOST NEEDED

O nce the 2015 Thanksgiving holiday was over, it was now time to clear the bar. We made a big promise when we said we would redefine the Super Bowl experience and that promise had massive stakeholder implications. It was time to get those plans into execution mode. Everything we did was going to be judged by critics everywhere, so we had to step it up.

Many of us went from getting several hundred emails to several thousand emails a day, and I don't mean collectively. Most staff members were now getting about a thousand emails, every single day. Sounds ridiculous, but it was true. Every minute of the day was precious, and that damn countdown clock just kept ticking away.

All at the same time we were launching, rolling out, promoting, fielding questions, meeting with stakeholders and putting the final touches on plans. We even managed to produce our own Host Committee magazine thanks to the stalwart efforts of our brand lead Whitney Hayes.

We were out in the market educating residents about everything from Super Bowl Week activities to commuter impacts to the app launch to partner programs to the latest 50 Fund grant opportunities. Our daily work with the NFL was increasing exponentially as their staff prepared to move here for the month of January. The valve on the fire hose never turned off.

It was stressful for sure but also exciting: it was time start unveiling the public experiences we had been working on for more than two years. We just had to keep our teams motivated over the coming weeks so we could get down the field and into the proverbial end zone.

STEPPING UP AS A LEADER

When immoveable deadlines approach and days get shorter, workloads explode and so too can the patience of your hardworking staff. This is the time when real leaders must step up because this is also the time when some team members—particularly those new to the task—can run the risk of falling apart.

As my wise friend Bill Campbell said: "Your title makes you a manager. Your people decide if you are a leader."

Having leadership and management skills are necessary in any successful venture, but there is a big difference between being a leader and being a manager.

» Leaders empower and mobilize their organization; they don't micro-manage them.

» Leaders encourage their teams to innovate and take calculated risks; they don't squash new ideas or diversity of thought.

» Leaders give their teams the credit for the accomplishment; they don't take the credit for themselves.

» Leaders look for criticism and differing opinions; they don't operate in a bubble.

» And when the days begin to get shorter on such a project, real leaders must show up.

Motivating a group of people to work tirelessly together requires more than the plan itself. Anyone can be a great speaker and rally the troops, but to ignite and continuously stoke the passion that is necessary to make a vision reality, it takes a real leader. We had two great role models in Daniel and Keith, our Chairman and CEO, and our team modeled that leadership behavior throughout our organization.

CARING FOR YOUR TEAM

When someone on your team is struggling, the team's leader owes it to everyone to step in. Whether it be professional or personal, adversity can come at unexpected times and from unexpected places; being an effective leader demands you act swiftly to help get that person back on track. This doesn't necessarily mean solving the problem for them, but instead providing coaching about possible paths forward or sometimes just being a sympathetic ear. It's also important to remember if you don't intervene, you not only let your struggling team member down, you let the rest of the organization down as well. By helping individual team members regain their footing, the team will recalibrate as well.

Having empathy for others is not a weakness, it's strength. Effective organizations demand commitment, focus and teamwork, but exceptional ones do all of that and adopt a culture where people look out for one another.

According to business management expert Tom Peters: "Management is about arranging and telling. Leadership is about nurturing and enhancing."

Creating an environment in which team members feel they have a safe space to turn problems into solutions is as much of an art as it is a science.

RECOGNIZING YOUR TEAM

The best—and most respected—leaders are usually more concerned with the success of the mission rather than receiving individual accolades. They are the ones who make their team members the heroes and are generous in recognizing the accomplishments of the team.

To make an impact, recognition needs to be public. It is important for leaders to acknowledge the ongoing contributions of team members individually, but being recognized in front of your peers delivers another level of satisfaction for employees.

This doesn't mean taking the approach of some youth sports leagues where all the children get a participation trophy no matter how the team did or how the child performed. To make recognition meaningful, it needs to be specific to the individual and show how his or her work made real contributions.

When our staff was large enough that we were splitting into departments, we began to host monthly All-Hands meetings to not only ensure every person was up to date, but also to provide the opportunity to recognize someone in front of the group. We formalized the process and created the "Team Member of the Month" award, recognizing one person's specific contributions in helping us to meet the organization's goals. While it seemed like a small thing to us, it was huge for the team, regardless of their years of experience. These moments helped us to thank our team members personally and publicly for their efforts, and reinforced the importance of each person's role in helping us to redefine the Super Bowl.

Since we like to say we are in the "fun business," we felt the recognition alone wasn't enough; we wanted to mark the occasion with a bit of fun as well. Upon my retirement from Major League Baseball, the San Francisco Giants had a special event for me at AT&T Park where every guest received a Pat Gallagher bobblehead they had specially made for the occasion. After the celebration ended, there were about 600 bobbleheads leftover from the bulk order, which were now sitting in my garage and multiple storage areas. I had absolutely no idea what to do with them until one of our senior leadership team members suggested we give each Team Member of the Month one as part of our recognition moments. We now had a no-cost award and it partially solved my ongoing bobblehead overpopulation problem; it was a double win.

It seemed like a silly thing to me, but the staff seemed to love getting my bobblehead as a symbol of their recognition. Even better, they proudly displayed them on their desks. My bobbling head was everywhere you turned in our Host Committee offices, but I predict eventually will wind up in garage sales or on eBay.

ACTIVE LISTENING

When I would speak publicly to groups and Bay Area residents about Super Bowl 50, I would always say "Super Bowl 50 is the first thing that the Bay Area has ever agreed upon" and then stop. This was usually met with a few moments of confused silence followed by laughter, because the notion that the Bay Area could agree on *anything* was ridiculous. We were 101 really different communities with very different needs and aspirations, and not lacking in opinion.

But that statement also often disarmed the room. It put everyone on notice that while we were confident in our overall plan, we knew in order to succeed, we would need to accept, respond and react to input, friendly or otherwise.

Successful leaders learn how to listen carefully to questions and input, and respond just as carefully.

As Stephen Covey said: "Most people do not listen with the intent to understand; they listen with the intent to reply."

One unintended result of these outreach efforts was that this approach helped us to humanize the event itself, even with some individual critics and skeptics as well. We weren't some faceless organization just doing what we wanted to do; we were their neighbors who actually wanted to hear their concerns and address them as best we could. It demonstrated we were willing to show up and listen as much as we talked.

We never wavered from our high-touch approach, even though constantly sharing the vision and elements of the plan as widely as we did felt downright exhausting at times. But we believed that communities around the Bay Area not only deserved to hear directly from us, but also have the opportunity to give us their input whether they agreed with us or not. There was no substitute for getting our face out there and really listening.

EMBRACING CRITICISM

Presenting an event with the size, scale and global attention of a Super Bowl can create enthusiasm, excitement and even passion, but it was also guaranteed to create skepticism, criticism and even a little fear. If you aren't getting criticized, it means you are doing something not worthy of criticizing. In other words: nobody cares. I'd remind others and myself on our team of this when the critics got loud, which they did at times.

In our case, we knew that public officials, electeds, opinion leaders, community groups and members of the media would all have opinions on how Super Bowl 50 should be run, and it was our responsibility to not only listen, but also to take action on these opinions as part of our planning process. These individuals not only had the right to interject, but also an obligation to their constituents to ask tough questions about how hosting a Super Bowl works and what that would mean for their communities.

When people share concerns, it's a good thing; criticism provides the opportunity to develop an even better plan. How an organization handles criticism, and the spotlight that comes with it, is just as important.

Dealing with the questions you can answer is a basic requirement; preparing your organization to anticipate and answer tough questions is what's important. It's when people are uninformed or ignored that problems can surface, and brushfires can quickly turn into conflagrations if not managed. Having the maturity and confidence to handle the situations you didn't see coming reveals real character.

KEY LESSONS

1. Effective leaders are people known not only for ability, expertise and determination, but also for their character. They are the ones who empower their teams, put the project objectives above personal needs and desires, and have the courage to fight for solutions, especially in times of uncertainty.

2. Having charisma is great, but it should not be confused with true leadership. Leaders motivate their teams not through pageantry and bluster, but by enabling team members to see how they play a critical role in the organization's success.

3. Taking the time to recognize and celebrate individual contributions can be an ingredient in the glue that holds a team together. For our team, recognition was not only a way to create a closer team, but also keep the energy of our team members high as the workload and pace increased.

4. By speaking about our plans with residents directly, we had the opportunity to not only share information, but also actively listen to their ideas and concerns. Criticism and constructive feedback provide great avenues for growth and improvement, but only if you show up and have open ears.

5. As a leader, you must always be prepared for criticism; it is a constant. How an organization responds to legitimate questions and concerns is an opportunity to earn the public respect, support and credibility everyone hopes to achieve.

CHAPTER 13

"USING TECH NOT ONLY FOR TECH'S SAKE"—THE SEARCH FOR RELEVANT TECHNOLOGY

B y 12:30 P.M. on January 29, 2016—the day before Super Bowl City opened—it was a full-on downpour. Not exactly what we had ordered for our media preview day.

Members of the media, our staff and our partners were gathered in the Fan Energy Zone, a giant 40-foot tall interactive dome that would serve as the heartbeat for Super Bowl City for the next week. In front of us, giant screens displayed video game-like images while lights of various colors flashed throughout the dome and arcade-style music played overhead. As our team prepared for the presentation, I took my normal spot at the back so I could watch the crowd's reaction to the show. I thought, we might have all been huddled together in an attempt to stay dry, but at least the electronics were working.

That thought occurred a few seconds too early. As San Francisco Mayor Lee strode up to join our other speakers, the presentation microphone went on the fritz. Here we were, about to talk about how Super Bowl City was built to be a celebration of the Bay Area's leadership in technology and innovation, and we get hamstringed by a simple blown fuse. You know what they say about the best-laid plans. Fortunately, the fix was quick and yet another reminder of why you have contingency plans for your contingency plans.

We held our collective breath for the rest of the presentation and made it through unscathed. Thanks to the massive job done by lead production partner e2k events x entertainment and partner SAP working with Britelite Immersive, Helios Interactive, Symmetry Labs and our crack Host Committee staff over the previous few days, the really important tech features all worked and were showtime ready for the fans. Forty-Niner player Torrey Smith and alum Steve Bono were able to demo the Fan Energy Zone games with relative ease, and the members of the media in attendance seemed genuinely interested in the interactive fan exhibits throughout Super Bowl City. All in all, it felt like a good start, though perhaps a bit of a wet one.

I stood back and took it all in as tours of Super Bowl City got underway post-presentation. The technology woven throughout Super Bowl City was a marvel to behold, especially to someone like me who remembered when the advent of fax machines was a huge advancement.

Innovation is in our DNA in the Bay Area, so it was important to us to use technology in useful and appropriate ways. It was also important to us that this wasn't just a display or showcase of tech for tech's sake. It had to be additive and not a distraction. It had to be core to what we were doing and not just a sideshow. And most importantly, it had to improve the fan experience, or it wasn't worth doing.

WEAVING TECHNOLOGY INTO OUR ORGANIZATION

Creating the most digitally advanced fan experience to date was one of our goals from the beginning; it started with putting our Super Bowl bid on Apple iPad minis and grew from there. It was never a question that technology would be incorporated into our Host Committee operations, but there was the question of how.

As an organization with a shelf life of two years and a tight scrutiny on where every dollar that would be spent, we had to be careful and only adopt what I referred to as "relevant technology."

To be useful to an organization, any piece of adopted technology has to offer a real solution to justify the investment.

As the anticipation of the Super Bowl grew in the marketplace, there were many sales teams out there eager to sell us on their technology, or provide us with free licenses or access. Because we live in an area where most of this stuff is being invented, we got to see amazing platforms and pretty some cool tools in all various stages of development. But being cool wasn't a key criterion for our search.

To determine what would work for us, we focused on finding tech solutions that were cost-effective, resource saving and could fulfill their promises. In other words, every solution had to be as reliable as the sun setting in the West, perform like a Maserati and as affordable as a Schwinn.

We were able to find tools that helped our organization to be nimble, save time, stretch our resources and even feed ourselves. On any given day, you might find a Host Committee team member issuing an invoice through Bill.com, sharing documents through

Box, uploading expenses through Expensify, taking an Uber to a meeting, entering a sales lead into our KORE database, reviewing click-through engagement through RadiumOne, answering their phone with Google VoIP, tracking story reach on our Zignal Labs dashboard, using Resumator to screen potential new hires, doing paperless evaluations of 50 Fund grants through Fluid Review or ordering lunch through Sprig. Thank goodness, we also had a strong IT partner in Langtech, because it was not pretty in our offices on the rare occasions the Wi-Fi went down.

Some of these tools came to us through our partners, and some through recommendations of peers and friends, but everything got passed through the same lens. As a temporary organization, free or discounted weren't good enough reasons to use a piece of technology. If the tool wasn't a true resource that helped us be more efficient with our time, staff and budgets, then we passed.

All of this efficiency caused me only minimal angst. As a baby-boomer who spent much of my adult life working life with rotary dial phones, yellow legal pads, and those pink "while you were away" phone message stickers, I was not instinctively comfortable using all of this technology. I credit my younger colleagues on the Host Committee, especially the always patient Nicole Carpenter, for showing me the way and calmly providing "tech-support" when I got stuck, which was often. I did, however, provide the acid test: if Pat could figure out how to use it, we could all figure it out.

DEVELOPING NEW SOLUTIONS

When you live and work in the Bay Area, you are surrounded by useful technology almost at every moment of the day, most of which is second nature to use. When it came to designing Super Bowl 50 fan experiences, we believed that would be a regional expectation as well.

We took the same approach as we did in building the digital venue finder with our website partner Channel 1 Media: determine the audience's need and work to improve it, just as we did by removing the need to lug around large binders of material.

To be useful, any fan-facing technology needs to put the fan squarely at the front of the design process.

According to Dan Saffer in his book *Microinteractions*, the combination of well-designed micro- and macro-interactions is a powerful one. "This is what experience design truly is: paying attention to the details as well as the big picture so that users have a great experience using the product."[19]

For example, we had a lot to communicate about Super Bowl City which meant developing a number of channels to reach different audiences, from our website to our social channels to traditional advertising and more. But how do we communicate to fans once they are onsite? How do we help them navigate the veritable wonderland of choices across our 10-acre fan village? Having enlisted Extreme Networks and PCM to help us deploy a reliable Wi-Fi network in Super Bowl City, we thought an event app was the no-brainer answer to those questions. Especially since practically every Bay Area event from SF Beer Week to the Half Moon Bay Art and Pumpkin Festival had an app. There had never been a Super Bowl app dedicated to the public fan experience, so we were starting from scratch. Step one: create the customer journey.

---

19   Saffer, Dan "Microinteractions" O'Reilly Media, 2013.

San Francisco would be home to Super Bowl City and the NFL Experience. Between the two, the 50th Mile, a mile-long natural corridor between the two sites on Market Street where the past 49 Super Bowls were celebrated with fan exhibits. (Fun fact: San Francisco is 49 square miles, so it made sense to add just one more, getting us to the creation of the "50th Mile." Sometimes the most obvious ideas are right in front of you.)

Building off the app we designed for the 50 Tour with our design partners Claremont Interactive and input from our friends at Google, our marketing communications team worked with NFL counterparts to identify:

» what information fans would need onsite to maximize their experience, from free concert schedules to exhibit information to maps with geo-location

» how fans would navigate our different footprints such as moving from one to the other, and what were the best ways to help fans to discover activities along the way

» the types of needs fans would have, such as finding food and drink, restrooms, official Super Bowl merchandise or our first aid stations provided by Kaiser Permanente

» information needed to help plan their experience, such as public transportation to visitor information to a personalized calendar

» how to serve up this information through a vehicle that could work for everyone

Designing with a fan-centric approach helped us to anticipate the needs of guests before they arrived.

Our objective was to make the Super Bowl City visit a great digital and analog experience for all guests, so we employed a number of traditional event resources, such as onsite signage, physical maps, volunteer ambassadors and mobile web. But with people spending 90% of their mobile time in apps[20], a dedicated event app provided us with an important added weapon for our arsenal.

CREATING A CONNECTIVE FAN EXPERIENCE

The delivery of a spectacular free public fan village was always a key part of our vision. As one of our "centers of gravity" during Super Bowl, it was a tangible expression of our brand promise so it needed to be more than a fair full of disparate amusements and attractions.

Our entire senior leadership team believed that Super Bowl City had to be designed as a truly interactive destination for people of all ages. From the minute fans walked through the gates, we wanted them to feel excited and encouraged to explore, play, taste, dance, cheer, laugh, sing, watch, enjoy and most importantly, understand that Super Bowl City was built for them.

To deliver the type of experience that could live up to the overall organizational vision, we had to be relentless in our pursuit of excellence.

All our partners understood what we were working towards, but to deliver this type of comprehensive fan experience, we needed to set early expectations, and provide very concrete guidelines and examples of what would and wouldn't work.

For example, for the sponsor and broadcast partners who were designing or having built an activation for Super Bowl

---

20   "How Americans Spend their Time on Mobile Devices" Flurry. 2015

City, we developed a design standard and asked our partners at MKTG to create associated brand guidelines to assist partners in their planning process. These materials helped partners look beyond their individual activations and understand they were part of the larger whole. The standard detailed our goal of creating a high-quality, unified fan experience which embraced sustainable practices, and how that could be accomplished through design, décor, branding, tone of fan communications, use of marks and material selection.

By formalizing the guidelines and communicating them to each partner and their contracted agencies well in advance, we were able to create an overall look and feel of a singular venue experience, while, at the same time, giving partners enough flexibility to allow their brands' individual personalities to come to life. Our goal was thoughtful brand integration, not our way or the highway.

We also highlighted the central theme that should thread throughout every experience—innovation—and that didn't just mean a technology display. As a region constantly curating, creating and collaborating on novel ways to better connect people to experiences and to each other, we wanted to showcase that core value. And our partners did not disappoint, with activations such as:

» An interactive football experience that let fans "take the field" for a final Big Game play from our Super Bowl City presenting sponsor, Verizon

» Virtual reality quarterback experience from SAP in addition to their work on the Fan Energy Zone and 40-foot interactive Fan Wall.

» 3D laser etchings of fans' faces onto glass cubes plus giving fans the chance to try out the latest in drone technology from Intel

» Nightly multi-story digital light show from Visa that transformed the sides of its headquarters building, which was adjacent to Super Bowl City

» Chevron's STEM ZONE where fans could explore how science, technology, engineering and math come to life through football

» Dignity Health's encouragement of fans to spread the simple but profound concept of humankindness through their digital campaign

» Kaiser Permanente's interactive and educational "2-minute drills" designed to be part of daily life to help improve overall health

» Human-powered selfie opportunities from Hyundai when fans generated the power through a touchdown dance

» Macy's two spectacular fireworks shows on the waterfront

» Levi's ultimate pop-up shop and elevated lounge, the perfect place to hang out and take in Super Bowl City

» A sustainably-built tasting lounge featuring hundreds of fine Sonoma County wines poured by the winemakers themselves

» A Golden Gate Bridge-inspired zipline and football catch from the CBS Sports Network

In designing something as complicated and with as many moving pieces as a fan village capable of hosting one million people, having a design standard enabled our staff to focus more of their time on where it should have been focused: on operation of Super Bowl City and the overall fan experience.

KEY LESSONS

1. While we wanted to be open to using the newest technology platforms available to help run our business, we were absolutely vigilant about vetting any purported tools. If a tool didn't save us time or money, or its use could impact our sanity, it wasn't a real solution.

2. To design something useful, we had to think about every step our guests would take, from first learning about the fan activities to going home at the end of the day. By thoughtfully mapping the customer journey, we were able to anticipate fan questions and proactively address their information needs.

3. By clearly communicating standards from the beginning, you enable partners to understand what is expected of them and how they can most effectively participate. In our case, creating a clear standard and expectation well in advance enabled our partners to create and deliver individual brand activations that were integrated parts of Super Bowl City, and did not appear to be just add-ons.

CHAPTER 14

"NO ONE WANTS TO KNOW HOW THE SAUSAGE IS MADE"—RESPONDING TO THE UNEXPECTED

During Super Bowl Week, we made a plan for our team leads to dial into a 30-minute operations update call each morning at 7:30 A.M., from wherever they were. Our second call was a doozy.

It was January 30, the first day of Super Bowl Week. Eighteen hours earlier, we had been hit with rain at the Super Bowl City media preview and now we were feeling the brunt of the cleanup. Today's plans had already called for the official opening of Super Bowl City, a morning press conference, operation of activations for a full 12 hours, and fireworks show and free concert to cap it all off, and now the already-long checklist had gotten longer. Our hard-working team was going to have to shift into another gear.

By 7:30 A.M., many on the call had been up most of the night. On the line, you could hear forklifts beeping in the background as Rosie Spaulding called in from her workspace above Justin Hermann Plaza, the site of Super Bowl City. With our crack event operations team leads John Mitchell and Michael Perlmutter on the ground, hundreds of contractors, vendors and partners were being mobilized for the day's activities. Kristi Calhoon led final preparations for our opening ceremonies, while Stephanie was putting the final touches on the opening remarks. Emma Lowenstein, our ace hospitality manager, prepared to open our media center lounge to thousands of visiting press, while our top-notch spokespeople—Nate Ballard, PJ Johnston, Joe Arellano and Kathryn Glickman—got ready to handle scores of interviews. It was all happening.

We were now in full execution mode and today's call was a reminder there was no more time left to plan; this was not a drill. Now, it was all about executing—as a team and with our multitude of partners—to the best of our ability what had been in the works for so many months, as well as being ready to deal with the unexpected in real-time.

THE SHOW MUST GO ON—MOVING ON WHEN THINGS GO WRONG

We had estimated at least a million people would pass through Bay Area Super Bowl public events based on the experience of previous host cities, but when you work in the events industry, there is always that niggling question spinning in the back of your brain: will they actually come?

We didn't have to wait long to find out. As our 7:30 A.M. call was under way, fans and residents were already checking out Super Bowl City before the attractions officially opened 2.5 hours later. Super Bowl City was a secure site, which meant visitors would have to go through a checkpoint before they entered the footprint, but it could be accessed at any time of day or night to not impede any commuters who were used to cutting across Justin Hermann Plaza on their way to work. By the time Keith and Daniel officially marked the opening of Super Bowl City at 11:00 A.M., the area was already teeming with fans. The feeling of excitement and anticipation was unlike anything I had experienced before.

There we were, right in the middle of Market Street, a bustling main corridor of San Francisco's downtown, that was now transformed into a series of multi-story exhibits, live performing arts and music performances, and local food and drink experiences. In front of me stood our main gate, an impressive black and gold structure that marked the start of the Super Bowl City journey for our guests. Flanking the opening of the gate were two dozen Host Committee volunteers, looking resplendent in their uniforms. The Gilroy High School Marching Band waited in the wings, ready to lead the crowd down to the main "bowl" of Super Bowl City. Our partners were gathered together by the giant 40-foot Fan Wall where we would soon play a video welcome from First Lady Michelle Obama. And, amazingly, the sun was shining.

As Daniel and Keith walked up to the podium—ready to welcome the thousands of fans now in front of us—I felt a swell of pride for what we were about to unveil with our extended family of public and private partners. In a break from Super Bowl tradition, we were about to open our public fan village four days earlier than had been ever done before. All of us felt it was important to give Bay Area residents the opportunity to experience the excitement of the Super Bowl before the majority of out-of-town fans arrived later in the week. To do that, we opened Super Bowl City and the NFL Experience the weekend before the Big Game, and planned activities that were designed specifically for locals, such as a free concert with Bay Area native Chris Isaak and the long-anticipated official re-lighting of the Bay Lights light sculpture on the Bay Bridge.

It was a whirlwind of a day that went on well into the night, but not everything went to plan. Our celebrity speaker had to drop out at the last minute. High winds overnight had untethered one of our displays inside one of the structures. A vendor spoke to a partner in a way that wasn't consistent with our values. An image appeared on our 40-foot digital Fan Wall that shouldn't have. Big events will always throw a few last-minute big curveballs, and we had to be ready to react quickly when the moment called for it.

Despite the best contingency planning, any event can quickly go awry. It's important to remember when the unexpected happens, quick thinking and a cool head are necessary to ensure the show goes on.

This is where having problem solvers versus problem creators on the team really pays dividends. Problem solvers take charge of the situation, make swift adjustments, look for the alternative path and stay calm.

No celebrity speaker? We just removed that part from the script. The swinging structure? We roped it off and got it firmly secured before the gates opened. The vendor? They were promptly let go and replaced. The image? We tightened up the process to ensure it wouldn't happen again.

You can't always fix the plans that have fallen through, but you can always move forward. And remember, the audience won't miss something they didn't know was supposed to be there in the first place.

MAKING THE TOUGH CALLS

Most people have no idea how much time and effort it takes to run a Super Bowl, nor frankly should they care. They care what they can see, the tip of the iceberg, not what is below the surface. As I like to say: "If we do this right, people will like the taste of the sausage, but no one wants to know how the sausage is made."

Now that Super Bowl Week was officially underway, we were up to our ears in sausage and serving it as fast as we could.

Being the maestros over the show isn't easy, which is why we focused on keeping the lines of communication open and flowing to solve any problems on the fly. With a central command center, radios plugged into every one's ear, mobile phones in hand and ongoing touch-base meetings happening throughout the day, our team leads made certain everyone was in the loop across our network of partners. Issues would be assessed, solved or escalated up the chain as necessary, and crisp decisions would be made, all in real-time.

During our second weekend—the weekend of the Big Game itself—we were now feeling the real crush of interest and excitement. The momentum was building each day. Those flying in for Super Bowl 50 were now in town, and word was fully out there that Super Bowl City was the place to be. Super Bowl City had now been open for five days and we were in a good swing with our operations, but we had seen more than 200,000 on our opening weekend alone. What would the final weekend look like when we projected the heaviest traffic coming through the footprint? We had to stand ready and stay vigilant. We had to anticipate, be ready, and prepare all the various partners down the line.

Chapter 14

Moments like this one is where the value of advance planning really came to the surface because there were no more dress rehearsals.

Similar to how we worked with the 30+ transit agencies around the region to develop the coordinated traffic management plan, we had also been planning with law enforcement stakeholders and other safety and security agencies for months. Intensive security planning for the game itself was nothing new; the League and its partners had been in a heightened state of planning for each Super Bowl since 9/11, working closely with the FBI and the Department of Homeland Security. But just two months prior to our Super Bowl Week, the world was rocked by deadly attacks in both Paris and San Bernardino. We were working on one of the most visible events in the world, so our security plans across the region were already tight, but now they had to become even tighter.

This is when the expertise of real seasoned professionals becomes most apparent. It would be impossible to adequately recognize every individual and every agency that stepped up during those final weeks of preparation for various public events. These are people who perform public safety duties every day without recognition and prefer it that way, seeing this painstaking work as professional responsibility. In our eyes, their dedication to this coordinated effort could only be described as extraordinary.

In particular, with Super Bowl City, the list is long and covers the San Francisco Mayor's Office, every department focused on public safety and security in San Francisco's City Hall and the Port of San Francisco, and representatives from local, state and federal public safety agencies. Like how we planned internally, every group had their piece of the puzzle and each piece was vitally important. Now they were doubling down on their efforts to ensure the safety and security of the public.

Both Friday and Saturday attracted the maximum crowds we anticipated, with more than 300,000 people coming through Super Bowl City. Hosting free concerts with One Republic and Alicia Keys, tied together with another Macy's fireworks show over the Bay and other fun, free activities proved to be an irresistible draw. As word came in from transit partners about the crowds making their way to our location throughout the day, we worked with the San Francisco Police Department, San Francisco Fire Department, other public agencies and our team to close the gates once Super Bowl City hit capacity and alert the public through multiple channels. Communication was swift and all partners executed their part of the closure plan with great care and diligence.

Reaching capacity was a double-edged sword. It was exciting that so many people wanted to be in Super Bowl City but we knew that some fans would be disappointed about not being able to get in. Ultimately, when you host a public event, the focus has to be on one thing—making the experience entertaining, organized and safe for everyone. Ensuring the safety of our guests was paramount to every one of our partners and none of us took that responsibility lightly.

OWNING YOUR MISTAKES

It is guaranteed, somewhere along the line, there will be mistakes made. No matter how much planning or preparation you do, a misunderstanding can occur, a ball can be dropped, a deadline can be missed, and reparations must be made.

Over the course of our two-year run, we made mistakes big and small. Some were internal, some were directly with partners, and some were more public. When any of our staff members made a mistake, we would naturally jump into problem-solving mode, but we also took the time to acknowledge what had happened.

No plan is perfect and mistakes are inevitable, but how you respond to those mistakes is what really matters.

When you make a mistake, one of the quickest ways to poison a partnership is to blame on it anything but yourself. An apology combined with a quick but thoughtful plan of action can engender confidence and credibility, while the wrong words can cause havoc. As Teddy Roosevelt said: "If you could kick the person in the pants responsible for most of your trouble, you wouldn't sit for a month."

Being dismissive, defensive or confrontational can destroy credibility and in our case, we had to keep confidence high that we would do the right thing. Laying blame not only doesn't solve the issue but also can, in many cases, further exacerbate the problem.

We believed, as an organization and as individuals, we were accountable for not only our decisions, actions and deliverables, but also accountable to our stakeholders. It was incumbent upon us to live up to our mistakes and work diligently to rectify the situation quickly and with our stakeholders in mind.

KEY LESSONS

1. As they say, expect the unexpected. Not everything will go to plan so while some things might be out of your control,

how you respond is not. By bringing in problem solvers versus problem creators, we were able to effectively anticipate and pivot in the moment instead of wallowing about what could have been.

2. Developing early partnerships not only results in a stronger, more integrated plan but also helps create the trust needed to handle critical situations and make tough decisions swiftly. In our case, those partnerships needed to be not only across agencies but also across jurisdictions, so maintaining open communication channels was vital to our joint success.

3. Making mistakes happens to everyone. By taking responsibility for your actions and working earnestly to fix mistakes, you not only have the chance to learn from your mistakes, but also keep the respect of your partners.

CHAPTER 15

"CLEANING UP AFTER THE ELEPHANTS"—TIME TO FULFILL OUR PROMISES

O
n February 8, 2016—the day after Super Bowl 50 was played at Levi's Stadium—we had our own Handoff ceremony in the NFL's media center. This time, those maniacally happy faces could be clearly seen on our team. More than two full years after we laid out the foundation for our organization, vision and values, Daniel, Keith and Jed York took the stage with their counterparts from the Houston Host Committee and NFL Commissioner Goodell. Now it was our time to hand off the ball.

Once the ceremonial footballs were gifted, the photos were taken and our Host Committee representatives had said a few words, Commissioner Goodell took time to publicly share his thoughts on Super Bowl 50.

"Everyone did an extraordinary job here to help stage a perfect celebration of Super Bowl. The leadership came together in a way we've never seen before and set a new bar for future host committees."

I don't think any of us could fully appreciate the meaning of those words as we were operating on fumes, but we definitely felt the gravity of the moment. The feeling was impossible to describe accurately: one part excitement, one part giant exhalation and one part growing realization this crazy ride was about to be over. And though our minds were now focused on the teardown process, each of us knew we have been part of something quite remarkable. Just as we had imagined from the start, there would much more left for our region than just cleaning up after the elephants once the circus left town.

INCORPORATING PURPOSE INTO PUBLIC EXPERIENCES

Our objective all along was to create experiences that were not only welcoming, exciting and engaging, but also reflected why we were hosting a Super Bowl in the first place: to benefit our people. Because we wanted to find ways to bring together people in our region, we made that emphasis foundational to what people would experience during Super Bowl Week. We wanted to bring that promise to life.

Super Bowl City itself was inherently designed to provide local fans and out-of-town guests alike the opportunity to come together in celebration around more than just football. Whether it was our Art Walk that promoted the work of Bay Area artists in collaboration with ArtSpan, or working local restaurateurs, food truck owners and Sonoma County vintners to serve food and wine with an emphasis on ingredients locally sourced, or staging more than 60 free performances featuring local Bay Area favorites, community performers and regional marching bands in addition to chart-topping headliners, we sought to provide experiences that would showcase the best of the Bay Area and appeal to a region with incredibly diverse tastes and interests. And of course, do it with a twinkle in our eye.

One of my favorite sights throughout Super Bowl Week was seeing the crowds lined up to take photos with our giant 18-foot tall 50 in the heart of Super Bowl City. Perfectly lined up with the San Francisco Ferry Building and its clock tower, also adorned with a 50, it proved to be *the* spot for taking a commemorative picture to share. But what I liked most about our big 50 was that it was more than just a photo op.

If you walked around to the side of the 50, you would find a walkway that would take you through the 50 and reveal hundreds of photos, videos and descriptions about the amazing nonprofits we were able to fund through the 50 Fund. Here on display was the real legacy of Super Bowl 50: faces of Bay Area children, youth and young adults who had benefited from the Host Committee's 50 Fund and the NFL Foundation's grant programs. We called it the *Faces of 50* and it served as our most visible reminder of our 50 Fund promise. It was important to us that the 1 million plus fans who came through Super Bowl City got to see not only how this Super Bowl could positively impact the lives of others, but also learn more about the hard-working nonprofits that are making real impact every day.

By the time Super Bowl Week rolled around, the 50 Fund had already given away $7.5 million to 141 high-performing local nonprofits, impacting more than 530,000 children across the Bay Area, and there was even more to come. By the time we were finished, the final number would cross the threshold of $13 million and would support the work being done by true community champions such as All Stars Helping Kids, CoachArt, Community Youth Center of San Francisco, GlobalGirl Media, Groundwork Richmond, Los Cenzontles Mexican Arts Center, Mo'Magic, the San Francisco LGBT Community Center, United Playaz and so many more. This was, as we promised, the most giving Super Bowl ever.

As our community relations team hosted our own programs and events in Super Bowl City and throughout the region—reading events, physical activity opportunities, celebrations of these nonprofit leaders, showcases of Business Connect partners—it was gratifying to see communities around the Bay Area hosting their own public events and recognitions of nonprofits. We all wanted to celebrate both the good work done by our neighbors and the legacy resulting from this seminal moment in time.

RETURNING TO NORMAL

Once the show was over, we had another promise to fulfill—getting venues and city streets returned to their normal operations as quickly as possible. What might surprise people is that even before Lady Gaga sang the first notes of the National Anthem inside Levi's Stadium, our wind-down was well underway.

While buses carrying thousands of fans, sponsors and media whisked down the Highway 101 to the stadium—including our own Fan Express led by the ever-enthusiastic Nicole Perkins—the load-out at Super Bowl City was in process, with similar cleanups and recycling of materials happening across Santa Clara, San Francisco and San Jose. As the players took the field, the decorations were coming down from event spaces, hotel lobbies, airports, public transportation and street poles.

Recycling and repurposing materials from our venues was just one of the ways we incorporated sustainable and responsible practices our daily operations, such as operating Super Bowl City on clean power thanks to PG&E. Working closely with the NFL and our sustainability advisor Neill Duffy, it took a deliberate plan and discipline to deliver on our promise of responsibly handling water, energy, waste, transportation and more to meet our "Net Positive" goals, but it was important that we walked the talk by embedding these practices throughout our work.

As the structures came down and game underway, many of our intrepid army of some 5,500+ volunteers were finished with their posts and had already returned to their civilian lives. With no official duty, they were now busy posting photos and connecting with other volunteers to re-live their stories about being a part of the Super Bowl 50 experience. Lasting friendships are created during moments like these and the stories will only get better with age.

Super Bowl City itself welcomed more than one million visitors over the course of nine days, and then came down in three-days' time. Our event operations leads and their extended teams worked around the clock to completely remove every vestige from the 10-acre site, re-open street closures and restore life as we knew it at the foot of Market Street and the Embarcadero in San Francisco as quickly as possible.

SHARING OUR GRATITUDE

We were privileged to work with some of the very finest people in the region—the inside-the-iceberg people like us who were dedicated to delivering their part of the plan—so for me and the others on our team, saying thank you was one of our very favorite Super Bowl 50 memories. Whether it was a fist bump with a volunteer, a handshake with a partner or a hug with a teammate, there was plenty of gratitude to share.

We'll fail if we try to mention all of them here, plus we know there are many who want their contributions to remain behind the scenes, so to the hundreds of people across the region who played roles big and small, please know how thankful we are for your partnership and always remember you helped create something that will have an impact for years to come.

In the days, weeks and months following the Super Bowl, all our Host Committee staff members took the time to spread our thanks far and wide. There were so many people to recognize, so many people who made Super Bowl Week and the entire lead-up possible. Our staff fanned out over the following months, making calls, paying visits, sending letters and giving out small tokens of appreciation to the thousands of folks who worked for us and together. And the greatest gift in return was when they shared a personal story about what was accomplished or how they felt appreciated for their efforts.

In my role as the lead for our corporate partnerships, thanking the partners—large and small—who invested not only their reputation, but also their resources, creativity and support was at the top of my list. In a region where there was no municipal spigot to turn on for events like the Super Bowl, there would have been no way the region could have paid for its obligations in the bid without private enterprise and private donations. Where possible, I visited them in person to look them in the eye, shake their hands (and hug most of them too) and share our sincerest thanks. The old-fashioned, personal gesture went a long way and allowed us, if even briefly, to celebrate all of this together.

Post-game, we followed up with each of our corporate partners to provide our wrap-up and the metrics from Super Bowl Week as well as ask for feedback—both good and bad. My final question to them: would they do it again? Almost all of them said yes, they would, and many even wanted to know how soon we could do it again. I smiled. Their satisfaction was good news indeed, but now, time for a vacation.

TAKING IT ALL IN

On February 9, 2016, our Host Committee team filed into the space at the Embarcadero Center we had been using as a volunteer command center during Super Bowl Week. We all crowded around over coffee and pastries, some of us seeing each other in person for the first time in weeks; there were stories, smiles and hugs all round. Super Bowl 50 was now over.

That morning served as an opportunity to reflect on the high points of the week that was now a blur. Keith and Daniel each shared their great pride in our collective work and how every one of our team had stepped up to create something that would not be forgotten any time soon. Our senior leadership team members each spoke about not only our accomplishments, but also how what we did was only possible because of the way we did it together. I felt myself choke up a bit as I looked around the room when it was my turn. I knew that what we had experienced was once-in-a-lifetime.

For the staff, the clock might have officially stopped counting down, but the work was not over. The complete wrap-up process lasts for many months after the conclusion of the game. But that morning together in the then-quiet volunteer command center on February 9, 2016 will stand out as a time when we felt real gratitude for our team and going through this experience together.

CHAPTER 16

"GIVING THE GAME AWAY"—WHY WE WROTE THIS BOOK

I n my final days of official duty working for the Host Committee after the Super Bowl had ended, I'd look forward to walking into our offices at 825 Battery. The inbox was more manageable, the incoming phone calls less frequent. The pulsing beat of the office and incessant buzz of activity had now left the building. We had shifted gears from driving flat-out to the finish line to a feeling that can only be described as a lot of satisfaction combined with a bit of relief. Plus, that infernal countdown clock was now permanently off, a respite but kind of sad at the same time.

There was still plenty to do to wrap it all up, but the pace was decidedly different, and certainly more humane. Stress was now replaced with smiles. Hugs were spontaneous. We swapped stories and shared laughter over moments and memories that only a fellow teammate could appreciate.

When Stephanie and I first talked about writing a book that would pull together our observations and perspectives from Super Bowl 50, we thought that an inside look at what we aspired to do and how it all came together might be of value and interest not only to those also in the "fun business," but also to anyone looking for some of the foundational elements that can make a business successful. Super Bowl 50 was, by any measure, the most visible and widely covered project in recent San Francisco Bay Area history, so we didn't want to just rehash what is already out there. Instead, we thought it would be more helpful to share some of the things from inside the iceberg with the hope of possibly inspiring others.

This certainly isn't the whole story; this book only scratches the surface of the San Francisco Bay Area Super Bowl 50 Host Committee's work on Super Bowl 50 and the contributions of the many, many people who were part of it. But giving all our strategies and secrets away would be akin to a football team giving their playbook to the opposition. We certainly would like to see another Super Bowl happen in this region's future so some of these strategies will have to stay on ice until the Bay Area is ready to bid again and create a new playbook. As I'd like to say when we discussed information not yet public around the office, we had to be prudent about sharing information with anyone outside of our Host Committee circle of trust so we didn't "give away the game." With this book, we've definitely given a peek inside, but we couldn't give it all away.

It will be a few years before the San Francisco Bay Area will have the opportunity to bid on another Super Bowl, but we believe with the results of Super Bowl 50, the region has more than earned its right to have that privilege once again, let alone pursue any big event it chooses. This experience demonstrated it is possible to unite this diverse region, find common ground for big ideas and bring communities together to do difficult but extraordinary things.

As we said to each of our staff members upon their hiring, if we succeed in realizing our vision, it would be something we would all share in, and an accomplishment we could be proud of for the rest of our lives. And for those who were "inside the iceberg" for the first time, it will be something that against which they can measure every future experience. I think it's safe to say every member of our Host Committee team is better because of the experience.

We also proved people of all ages and expertise could come together to make something spectacular. I was, by far, the most senior person at the Host Committee in terms of age and previous experience. I would often joke my primary role was to provide "adult supervision." The other members of our staff seemed to enjoy or at least put up with most of my points-of-view and familiar sayings, and if they didn't, they were too polite to tell me. But what I will remember most about this team is how each member stood shoulder-to-shoulder in support of not only a dream, but also of each other.

In any complicated endeavor, there are times when things just don't go right and we definitely had some of those times. There will be roadblocks, difficult people who will stand in your way, good people who just don't agree, not enough money to do everything you would like to do, and your phone calls just won't seem to get returned. There are times when you just need a "yes" and all the best you can get is a "no," or even worse, a "maybe." If you are persistent and keep your cool, a "no" today can sometimes become a "yes" down the road. So, if the clock is ticking away and you find yourself and your organization just plain stuck, don't give up.

One of the biggest lessons that come out of doing something difficult is learning to soldier on when the going gets really rough. That is when you discover the true character of the organization you work for, the people you work with and what you as a person are made of. Every single person who was part of the Host Committee experienced some issue or problem along the way, and some more than others. We needed the courage to act not only swiftly, but also in line with the values we set out at the beginning.

In the end, we proved to ourselves it is possible to shoot for the stars. Our small group of original members declared from the very beginning not only what we would do, but also how we would go about it. Deciding what you stand for, who will you allow onto your team and how you will treat people along the way are principles not reserved for putting on a Super Bowl, they are the ingredients of any successful endeavor.

We worked hard to stay true to our vision and values every step of the way. It certainly didn't make our path any easier, and sometimes, it resulted in a whole lot more work, but by not compromising, the result was a better end product for everyone. By staying true to our vision, we were able to deliver our main objective: leaving a true legacy of positive impact throughout the San Francisco Bay Area.

CHAPTER 17

SUPER BOWL 50 BY THE NUMBERS

denotes Super Bowl record

MOST GIVING:

Our 50 Fund and its partner organizations raised more than $13 million to help close the opportunity gap for low-income children, youth and young adults living in the Bay Area.

» $13 million donated*

» 537,000 youth and families living in low-income communities benefitted from the 50 Fund grants*

» 141 nonprofits in 12 counties received a 50 Fund grant*

» 103,000 books distributed through The Re(a)d Zone*

» 27,107 Net Positive pledges taken as part of the Play Your Part campaign

» 28,500 trees planted as part of the NFL Urban Forestry program

» 84% of Bay Area residents agreed it is important for major events to give back to the community

MOST SHARED:

Super Bowl 50 set digital and social media records across the board.

- » First-ever public fan experience app
- » 4.3 billion views of Super Bowl content*
- » 155 million fan interactions on Instagram*
- » 330 million views of Super Bowl ads on YouTube*
- » 13.9 million Snapchat story views on Super Bowl Sunday*
- » 141 million fan interactions on Facebook during Super Bowl Week
- » 3.1 million social media impressions related to the 50 Tour
- » 9+ billion total media impressions*
- » 167.0 million viewers, making it the most-watched single broadcast in television history to date*
- » 3.96 million unique viewers across devices*
- » 7 terabytes of data transferred over the Super Bowl City Wi-Fi network*
- » 30 terabytes of data used by Verizon customers in Super Bowl City*
- » 10.1 terabytes of data transferred over the Levi's Stadium Wi-Fi network*
- » 15.9 terabytes of data transferred over the Levi's Stadium Distributed Antenna System*
- » 27,316 unique and 20,300 concurrent Wi-Fi users at Levi's Stadium on Super Bowl Sunday*
- » 11.7 million page views of the Host Committee's website*
- » 5.9 million total visitors to the Host Committee's website*

» 4.8 million unique visitors to the Host Committee's website*

» 149,000 unique followers of Host Committee social channels*

MOST PARTICIPATION:

Participation meant more to our team than just the opportunity to attend an event; we wanted this Super Bowl to be more inclusive and offer more opportunities for local businesses and communities to benefit and celebrate.

» 1.9 million Bay Area adults attended at least one Super Bowl Week event, which is one third of our region's population

» 1,350 business owners attended a Business Connect workshop

» 435 diverse local companies participated in Business Connect

» 66 Bay Area communities participated in the first-ever Super Communities program

» 864 applications for a 50 Fund Game Changer or Playmaker grant

» 550,000 fans interacted with the 50 Tour, which visited 18 cities in 11 counties over 3 months

» 85% of event attendees gave Super Bowl 50 a high-performance rating

ECONOMIC IMPACT:

Super Bowl 50 provided a positive net economic impact to the Bay Area of at least $240 million, which was the amount spent by non-local game and Super Bowl event attendees, and spending by event organizers on logistics and operations. The $240 million number included only spending considered to be directly spurred by the Big Game and did not include spending that was likely displaced during this time period, so spending by Bay Area residents during Super Bowl week was largely excluded.

» $240 million net positive economic impact on the Bay Area

» $194.3 million spent by out of town visitors

» $6.1 million in NFL and Host Committee contracts won by Bay Area diverse businesses*

» $8.2 million in hotel tax generated in San Francisco February 5-7, an increase of more than $5.3 million and a 190% increase YOY*

» San Francisco International Airport concessionaires saw $4.6 million in incremental revenue during Super Bowl Week

» 64% of adults said it is important to host major sporting events in the Bay Area. Respondents cited the importance of job creation, economic benefits, legacy impacts, community spirit and pride, and the promotion of the Bay Area as a tourist destination globally.

SUPER BOWL CITY PRESENTED BY VERIZON:

» 9 days

» 1.1 million visitors

» 64 free performances on The City Stage presented by Levi's

» 17,629 immersive game sessions by fans from 34 states and 6 countries in the Fan Energy Zone presented by SAP

» 20,000 glasses of Sonoma County wine served

VOLUNTEERS:

» 5,500 volunteers

» 100,000 volunteer hours

» 15,000 volunteer shifts

» 2,507 community services hours

NET POSITIVE:

The Host Committee made a commitment early in the planning process to deliver Super Bowl 50 as a Net Positive event, which meant leveraging Super Bowl 50 as a platform to do good for the entire Bay Area—socially, environmentally and economically.

» Three volunteer uniform items (polo, half zip, hat) were made entirely from recycled PET and 50% of uniforms were made from recycled materials

» 67 million BTUs of energy saved by using recycled content in volunteer uniforms

» Electric buses were incorporated in the fleet used to transport media

» Super Bowl City operated on PG&E clean power, with 91% of temporary power supplied by Neste renewable diesel generators and 2% of power from hydrogen fuel cell generators

» The Host Committee offset 300mT of their Scope 1 and 2 residual emissions through our work with TerraPass

» The Host Committee's master concessionaire served locally-sourced (within 75 miles) or organic food in Super Bowl City

» 860 pounds of Super Bowl City food was recovered and donated to local food banks through Food Runners

» Sustainable product use in Super Bowl City included 162,000 compostable cups, 10,000 bamboo boats/plates, 9,000 eco-friendly cups, 5,000 eco-friendly disposable plates and 3,000 wine glasses

» No single-use plastic bottles were served to fans in Super Bowl City

» Free water filling stations in Super Bowl City delivered 1,925 gallons of water, the equivalent of eliminating 14,580 single-use plastic bottles from landfill.

» 119 tons of material and event waste from Super Bowl City was diverted from landfill

» 80 resources recovery stations were available at NFL and Host Committee venues that captured 25,000 lbs. of material to reuse, 15.5 tons of compost/organics, 66.6 tons of recyclables, and 40.8 tons of trash of which 66% of the tonnage was recyclable.

TRANSIT:

Over 30 regional transit providers and partners collaborated to enable residents and guests to travel safely, sustainably and as easily as possible around the Bay Area during Super Bowl Week.

- » 3.4 million people rode BART, with February 6, 2016, being its busiest Saturday in its history
- » 69,000 people took the SF Bay Ferry, a ridership increase of 81%
- » 200,000 extra subway trips on Muni were taken
- » 1.2 million travelers came through the San Francisco International Airport, an increase in 15.7%
- » 40,000 Uber careshare trips with riders from 314 cities and 58 countries
- » 9,500 people rode VTA on Super Bowl Sunday to Levi's Stadium
- » 48% increase in ridership on Caltrain during Super Bowl Week
- » 856 bikes parked at the Super Bowl City bike valet

January 31, 2015. Host Committee Handoff Ceremony at Super Bowl XLIX in Arizona, with Host Committee Chairman Daniel Lurie, 49ers CEO Jed York, and Host Committee CEO Keith Bruce (left to right)

August 31, 2015. In his role as Host Committee EVP of marketing, communications and partnerships, author Pat Gallagher gets ready for the official opening of the 50 Tour during NFL Kickoff in San Francisco.

November 17, 2015. A special visit by NFL Commissioner Roger Goodell and 49ers CEO Jed York to the Host Committee's San Francisco offices.

November 21, 2015. Host Committee team joins the 50 Tour stop in Sausalito, CA. The 50 Tour visited 18 cities across the Bay Area over two months, and reached more than 550,000 fans.

January 30, 2016. Author Stephanie Martin, at the entrance of the Host Committee's Super Bowl City, prepares for the grand opening ceremony in her role as vice president of marketing and communications.

January 30, 2016. Fireworks celebrate the opening night of Super Bowl City. In the foreground, the giant 50 serves up the ultimate photo op, while inside, it tells the story of some of the Bay Area's most impactful nonprofits.

February 3, 2016. The City Stage comes to life. Super Bowl City hosted more than 60 free performances during Super Bowl Week.

February 6, 2016. Super Bowl City, the Host Committee's free-to-the-public fan village, saw more than 1 million fans over the course of nine days.

ACKNOWLEDGMENTS

The development of *Big Game, Bigger Impact* was a true passion project, so we'd like to thank Justin Sachs and the Motivational Press team for helping us bring it to life. We are very grateful.

We'd also like to thank those who read the many drafts of this book, and helped us jog our memories along the way. Your comments and commas were vital to the process, as well as your words of encouragement and support. Thank you Danielle DeLancey, Joan Gallagher, Brian Keefe, Bob Keefe, Linda Keefe, Mike Martin, Lizz Ogletree, Rosie Spaulding, Mimi Towle and Jason Trimiew.

So many people were instrumental in the making of *Big Game, Bigger Impact* because, at its heart, this book is about how people from around the Bay Area came together in partnership to redefine the Super Bowl experience and ensure its legacy would be felt long after the last whistle was blown. What follows isn't an exhaustive list as there were thousands of people who came together to make Super Bowl 50 possible, but includes some of people with whom we worked with directly, and to whom we owe great thanks and gratitude for their partnership.

First, we'd like to recognize each of our amazing teammates from the San Francisco Bay Area Super Bowl 50 Host Committee. We are blessed to have had this opportunity to work together and think of you all as family: John Amore, Sarah Louise Atkinson, Gina Beltrama, Keith Bruce, LaMecia Butler, Kristi Calhoon, Nicole Carpenter, Kyle Chank, Danielle DeLancey, Oliver Divljak, Walt Dobrowolski, Tyler Ffrench, Chris Garrity, Sarah Hawkins, Whitney Hayes, Arielle Johnson, Danaeya Johnson, Elle Kehoe, Emma Lowenstein, Alissa May, John Mitchell, Nicole Perkins, Michael Perlmutter, Kevin Solon, Rosie Spaulding, Ken Tamura, Jason Trimiew, Michelle Villanueva, Vicky Wijsman and Jesse Yeager.

To our chairman Daniel Lurie for seeing the potential for the Big Game to be a platform for good and how it could make a lasting impact on our community. Thank you for entrusting us with the responsibility to bring your vision to life; we hope we've made you proud.

To our CEO Keith Bruce for setting the tone for our entire organization, and challenging us every day to create something great on behalf of our region. Thank you for bringing this team together and inspiring us to set the bar a little higher every day.

To Mayor Ed Lee of the City and County of San Francisco, and San Francisco 49ers Jed York for making it possible to bid on Super Bowl 50. Thank you for creating an opportunity that has benefitted so many throughout our region.

To our partners at the National Football League, true professionals who were also true partners, we were privileged to have worked with you: Peter O'Reilly, Angela Alfano, Renie Anderson, Mary Pat Augenthaler, Ana Blinder, Mark Brady, Tom Brady, Brittany Branscomb, Alison Byrne, James Carmichael, David Cohen, Alison DeGroot, Maggie Delmoral, Brett Diamond, Nicki Ewell, Eric Finkelstein, Alexia Gallagher, Alex Gerson, Jack Groh, Susan Groh, Lisa Heckman, Amanda Herald, Dave Houghton, Christina Hua, Cindie Hurley, Anna Isaacson, Matt Kallinger, Katie Keenan, Michael Koval, Ashley Leavens, Jessica Lee, Peter Locke, Victoria Loughery, Aidan Lyons, Mimi MacKinnon, Rachel Margolies, Brian McCarthy, Shandon Melvin, Heather Nanberg, Christine Mills, Max Paulsen, Tracy Perlman, Ashton Ramsburg, Kelsy Reitz, Melissa Schiller, Jennifer Scuteri, Matt Shapiro, Carly Slivinski, Dave Shaw, Michael Signorino, Doug Smoyer, Chris Stackhouse, Frank Supovitz, Mark Waller, Daphne Wood and Nancy Wygand, as well as Wayne Kostroski from the Taste of the NFL, Steve Brener and the team at Brener Zwickel & Associates, Pat Ryan and the PPW team, Cristine Paull and Mike Witte of SP+Gameday, RJ Orr and the team at Blue Media, and Jerry Anderson, Todd Barnes and the Populous team.

To our incredibly talented and motivated associates who showed us every day that it is not your years of experience, but rather your passion and drive that make all of the difference: Camila Borsato, Alyssa Carrion, Elaine Cleland, Skylar Corcoran, Christopher Doherty, Justine Dutton, Travis Gorsch, Alex Johl, Madeleine Kerr, Tyler Kingsley, Alena Kleinbrodt, Heather Luna, Mackenzie Murtagh, Kathryn Petkevich, Sheridan Spivey, Kloi Terzian, Chris Tesoriero, Michelle Watt, Taylor White, Taylor Williamson, Lauren Winkelman and Kayla Wonderly.

We'd also like to thank our partners and advisors who felt like real members of the Host Committee team, and worked with us shoulder-to-shoulder throughout this experience. Their contributions were critical to our success and their fellowship made it even more fun: Joe Davis, Drake Watten and our team of Boston Consulting Group associates; Evan Karasick, Rick Amos and Bill Avgerinos of Channel 1 Media; Neal Pollock and Conor Pollock of Claremont Interactive; David Perry and Alfredo Casuso of David Perry & Associates; Stewart McDowell, Matt Berde and Danny Mandel of Gibson Dunn; Phi Tran of Langtech; Chip Nilsen of Nilsen Architecture & Planning; Michael Schwab and Carolyn Gustely at Michael Schwab Studios; Neill Duffy of Purpose & Sport; Ken Tamura, Zach Little and Blake Warner of Silicon Valley Partners; Marisa Giller at Tipping Point; Wes Wernimont of WesWer Design; David Berger, T.J. Graham and Lixian Hantover of Wilson Sonsini; and communications strategists Joe Arellano, Nate Ballard, Kathryn Glickman and PJ Johnston.

To our fantastic Board of Directors who helped guide us every step of the way, we could not have done this without you: Joe D'Alessandro, Rodney Fong, John Goldman, Daniel Lurie and Becky Saeger.

A great thank you to our 50 Fund Board of Directors and those who supported the mission of the 50 Fund through the gracious contribution of their time: Aida Alvarez, David Berger, Fred Blackwell, Lydia Beebe, Megan Garcia, Stephen Green, Michele Lew, Daniel Lurie, Lenny Mendonca, Vincent Pan, Yvette Radford, Carmen Rojas, Kamba Tshionyi, Lauran Tuck, Briana Zelaya, as well as actor Peter Coyote for lending his voice to our 50 Fund video, and to those who directly supported the 50 Fund with significant donations including Bill Campbell, Bruce Dunlevie, Fred Harman, Jesse Rogers, John Goldman and a few others who prefer to be anonymous.

To our Host Committee Advisory Group, which included some of the leading innovators in their respective fields, all of whom were united in their love for the Bay Area and the opportunity that came with hosting a Super Bowl. We could not thank them enough for their time, talent and trust. Thank you to Nikesh Arora, Robert Mailer Anderson, Azania Andrews, Gwyneth Borden, Mayor Willie Brown, Quentin Clark, James Curleigh, Joe Davis, Lloyd Dean, David Drummond, Mayor Gary Gillmor, Ron Gonzales, Carl Guardino, John Hinshaw, Greg Johnson, Thomas Keller, Chris Kelly, Thomas Klein, Brian Krzanich, Stephen Luczo, Paraag Marathe, Marissa Mayer, Kevin Moore, Mary Murphy, Matt Prieshoff, Larry Renfro, Condoleezza Rice, Charles Schwab, George Seifert, Bruce Sewell, Charlotte Shultz, Brad Smith, Larry Sonsini, Bernard Tyson, Jeff Ubben, Michael Wirth, Jim Wunderman, Steve Young and Gideon Yu.

We were fortunate to work with some of the greatest professional football current players and alumni, men whose achievements on the field, and philanthropic and community efforts off the field could only be described as heroic: Anquan Boldin, Steve Bono, Fred Biletnikoff, Dennis Brown, Raymond Chester, Dwight Clark, David Diaz-Infante, Ted Kwalick, Ronnie Lott, Guy McIntyre, Joe Montana, Keith Moody, Lorenzo Neal, Bubba Paris, Jim Plunkett, Eason Ramson, Jerry Rice, Jesse Sapolu, Dana Stubblefield, Justin Tuck, Ricky Watters, Eric Wright and Steve Young.

To the staff members of the San Francisco 49ers and the Oakland Raiders for being such incredible teammates and supporters, as well as entrusting us to take care of their Lombardi Trophies. We are truly thankful for the partnership of Marc Badain, Rosie Bone, Morris Bradshaw, Brandon Doll, Will Kiss Jerry Knaak, Tyler Moorehead, Kelly Stein, Mike Taylor and Erin Wright at the Oakland Raiders; and Robert Alberino, Mike Anderson, Ethan Casson, Angele Cory, Dan Cory, Al Guido, Roger Hacker, Bob Lange, Jesse Lovejoy, Paraag Marathe, Jim Mercurio, Krista Olson, Joanne Pasternack, Ted Robinson, Bob Sargent, Ali Towle, Keena Turner and Tony Vroman at San Francisco 49ers.

A great thank you goes to the organizations that helped fuel the Host Committee and our vision, and to the people who became real partners in our effort including Anheuser-Busch's Eelco van der Noll, Anna Rogers, Tom Haas and Dick Unsinn; Apple's Tim Cook, Bruce Sewell, Joanie Morgado, Greg Joswiak and Phil Schiller; Boston Consulting Group's Joe Davis, Drake Watten, Erica Carlisle, Suchi Sastri and Jordan Levy; Chevron's Mike Wirth, Gail Joerger, Tricia Regan, Melissa Ritchie, Glenn Weckerlin, Steve Woodhead and Steve Green; Dignity Health's Lloyd Dean and Wade Rose; Extreme Networks' Norman Rice; Gap's Bill Chandler, Margot Shaub, Kari Shellhorn, Debbie Mesloh, Liz Krukowski and Emily Russell; Google's Nikesh Arora, David Drummond, Matt Hirst, Michaela Prescott, Ben Quesnel and Lorraine Twohill; HP/HPE's Meg Whitman, Todd Bradley, Cyndie Wang and John Hinshaw; Intel's Paul Ottolini, Brian Krzanich, Kari Lemiere and Penny Baldwin; Intuit's Brad Smith, Greg Johnson and Caroline Donahue; Kaiser

Permanente's Bernard Tyson, Yvette Radford and Jennifer Scanlon; KORE's Todd Cusolle; Levi's Chip Bergh, James Curleigh, Stacy Doren, Mark Foxton, Curtis Hanlon and Becca Prowda; Macy's Amy Kule; Optum's Larry Renfro; Pebble Beach's Mark Ferland and Tim Ryan; PG&E's Rob Black; SAP's Chris Burton, Dan Fleetwood, Ward Bullard and Kathleen Murray; Seagate's Scott Horn, Steve Luczo and Michael Busselen; Uber's Amy Friedlander; ValueAct Capital's Jeff Ubben, Kelly Barlow and Briana Zelaya; Verizon's Monique Harrison, Steve Parry, Eric Reed and Kristin Rooney; Virgin America's David Cush and Sabine Middlemass; Visa's Chris Curtin and Lara Potter; Yahoo's Marissa Mayer and Ken Goldman.

To our fantastic media partners for helping us to invite residents from across the region to experience Super Bowl 50 in their own backyard: Bruno Cohen, Chris Flynn, Doug Harvill, Mike Martin and the entire KPIX/KCBS team; William Burton, William Patterson and the KGO/KABC team; Rich Cerussi, Jordan Knopf and the KNTV/NBC Bay Area team; Tony Cafarelli and the Entercom team; iHeart Radio's Katie Wilcox, Don Parker and Val Klein; Lee Hammer, David Drutz and the KNBR team; Ashley Morris, Bob Hall, Anna Baird, Mike Werner and Luis Aguilar of RadiumOne; Sarah Leary and Kelsey Grady at Nextdoor; Outfront Media's Kyle Henley, Clear Channel's Bob Schmitt and Joe Cunningham; Chloe Hennen, Natalie Wages and the 7x7 team; Erika Brown and the entire team of the Bay Area News Group; Betty Sullivan and the San Francisco Bay Times; Mary Huss and the San Francisco Business Times team; and Jeff Johnson, Sarah Morse, Brandon Ramirez and the staff at the San Francisco Chronicle and SFGATE. We'd also like to recognize the tremendous community of journalists we are lucky to have in the San Francisco Bay Area.

To our live event partners who helped bring the Super Bowl 50 dream to life in such spectacular fashion: Mohamed Ahmed and the Admiral Security team; John Flores, Lynda Greenberg, Oliver McGinnis and the Britelite Interactive team; Allison Carnes-Staley and the Blueprint Studios team; photographer Christopher Dydyk; Michael Olmstead, Jason Greenberg, Mike Brady, Andy Bergdahl and the entire e2k events x entertainment team; Goodby Silverstein's Rich Silverstein, Michael Crain, Chris Nilsen and Luke Dillon; Bob Sarut and Denny Walch at Legends Hospitality; Matt Prieshoff and the entire Live Nation team; MKTG's Patty Hubbard, Rob Deal, Eric Evenson, Nick Bryden, Derek Cummings, Nikhil Parsad, Bree Brooks, Wayne Dull, Tim Staley and Brian J.; Cristina Gastelu-Villarreal and the entire Seasons team; Gerry Rubin and the entire Sitelines team; Alan McIntosh and the team at Way to Be; Zignal Labs' Tim Murray and Tim Hayden, and all of the contractors who joined our staff and became part of our family.

The incredible professionals of the Bay Area and California tourism industry including San Francisco Travel's Joe D'Alessandro, Patricia Aleman, Laurie Armstrong, Jon Ballestreros, Lynn Bruni, Lisa Cleveland, Erin Rheinschild, Paul Frentsos, Ernie Garcia, Tyler Gosnell, Lisa Hasenbalg, Kathryn Horton, Cindy Hu, Lysa Lewin, Deirdre Lewis, Terry Nguy, Todd O'Leary, Leonie Patrick, Howard Pickett, John Reyes and Tina Wu; Sonoma County's Ken Fischang, Mark Crabb, Honore Comfort, Charmaine Louzao, Karissa Kruse and Carolyn Stark; Visit California's Carolyn Beteta and Lynn Carpenter; Napa Valley's Clay Gregory, Stacey Dolan and Angela Jackson; Steve Van Dorn, David Andre, Lisa Moreno and Annette Manhart of the Santa Clara Convention and Visitors Bureau; Team San Jose's Laura Chmielewski, Ben Roschke, Karolyn Kirchgesler, Jennifer DeForest and Meghan Horrigan; Christine Bohlke at Marin Convention & Visitor's Bureau; San Francisco Hotel Council's Kevin Carroll and Kelly Powers; Visit Oakland's Alison Best, Kim Bardakian and Frances Wong; and Visit Tri-Valley's Barbara Steinfeld and Emmy Kasten.

To the universities who hosted the two Super Bowl 50 contenders at their facilities, thank you for your partnership: Gene Bleymaier, Marie Tuite, Lawrence Fan, Mike Waller and Matt Miller of San Jose State University Athletics Department; and Bernard Muir, Jamie Breslin and Maggie Fenton of Stanford University.

Members of the San Francisco Bay Area business community who lent their skills and expertise, and allowed us to bend their ears: Donna Armstrong, Kevin Bartram, Richard Bulan, Ron Conway, Ben Davis, Sharan Dhanoa, Dr. Suzanne Giraudo, Karin Flood, Rufus Jeffris, Nan Keeton, Tom Klein, Jim Lazarus, David Lewin, Bob Linscheid, Joen Madonna, John Marks, Susie McCormick, Paul Pendergast, Bob Pester, Dick Shaff, Pete Sittnick, Ron Tumpowsky, and all of the members of our Arts & Culture, Communications, Hospitality, Sustainability and Volunteer committees. In addition, we'd like to recognize our Super Bowl City neighbors for their tremendous support and partnership including Bob Pester and Boston Properties; Philip Johnson and the Federal Reserve; Jane Connors and the Ferry

Building; Antoine Berberi and the Hotel Vitale; David Lewin and the Hyatt Regency San Francisco; Jose Guevara and the Landmark Building; Norm Dito and One California; Christine Mann and One Market; and Rob Black and PG&E.

Thank you to our great friends in the Bay Area sports and events community for always being just a phone call away: Zennie Abraham, Larry Baer, Andy Dallin, Chrissy Delisle, Andy Dolich, Cassie Hughes, Sara Hunt, Jan Katzoff, Amy Knop, Adam Lippard, Michael O'Hara Lynch, Jason Pearl, Carmen Policy, Stephen Revetria, Ted Robinson and Beth Schnitzer, as well as thank you to industry-groups BASE and WISE Bay Area for your support.

A special thank you goes to the members of the broader Super Bowl Host Committee family and those who went before us: Indianapolis' Allison Melangton; New York/New Jersey's Al Kelly, Mark Bingham and Amy Blumkin; and Arizona's Jay Parry, Jeramie McPeek and Kathleen Mascarenas.

To the 5500+ people who took time away from their daily lives to join us on this journey as volunteers, we are eternally grateful. You were true ambassadors of the Bay Area. We'd like to tip our hats to a few volunteers with whom we worked closely: MaryAnne Drummond, Renee Hamilton-McNealy and David Torres.

To the teams at the more than 150 nonprofits who were 50 Fund awardees, for inspiring us with your commitment to the community and reminding us that every individual can make a difference.

To the more than 400 minority-owned, women-owned, LGBT-owned and disabled veteran-owned businesses in our Super Bowl 50 Business Connect program who are a testament of the vibrant, diverse and supremely-skilled business community of the Bay Area.

To the hundreds of people with whom we worked from federal, state, city and community governmental agencies across the region, we are incredibly thankful for your time and unflagging effort. Below, we've recognized some of these people and the organizations with whom we had the great pleasure and privilege of working with directly.

From the City and County of San Francisco: Mayor Ed Lee and the incredible team from the Mayor's office including Steve Kawa, Tony Winniker, Jason Elliott, Christine Falvey and Francis Tsang; the San Francisco Board of Supervisors; Chief Greg Suhr, Deputy Chief Mike Redmond and the entire San Francisco Police Department; Chief Joanne Hayes-White and the entire San Francisco Fire Department; Director Monhammed Nuru and the staff of SF Department of Public Works; Director Monique Moyer and her team at the San Francisco Port; Director Ed Reiskin, Candace Sue and the SFMTA entire team; General Manager Phil Ginsburg and the staff of Rec and Park; Executive Director Anne Kronenberg and the staff of Department of Emergency Management; Director of Convention Facilities John Noguchi; Director Todd Rufo and the OEWD team; Executive Director Regina Dick-Endrizzi and the Office of Small Business team; John Martin and his team at SFO; Tim O'Brien at SFO Museum; Director Carla Johnson and the Mayor's Office on Disability;

Dr. Emily Murase and the Department on the Status of Women; Susan Robbins and the staff at the SF Film Commission; Tom DeCaigny and the team with SF Arts Commission; Jocelyn Kane, Audrey Joseph and the SF Entertainment Commission team; and the incomparable Martha Cohen for whom we thank for her incredible partnership and great friendship.

From the City of Santa Clara: Mayor Jamie Matthews; Mayor Lisa Gillmor; the Santa Clara City Council; Santa Clara City Manager Julio Fuentes; Assistant City Managers Ruth Shikada, Alan Kurotori and Sheila Tucker; Communications Director Jennifer Yamaguma; Director Jim Teixeira and the of Parks & Recreation staff; Director of Information Technology Gaurav Garg; Santa Clara City Librarian Hilary Keith; Chief Mike Sellers, Capt. Phil Cooke, and the entire Santa Clara Police Department; Chief William Kelly and the entire Santa Clara Fire Department; John Southwell of the Santa Clara Marriott, and Santa Clara sponsorship and fundraising consultant Peggy Kennedy. In addition, we'd like to thank the City of Santa Clara Super Bowl 50 Marketing Committee members for their great partnership including Santa Clara City Councilmember Debi Davis, Santa Clara University's Butch Coyne, Great America's Roger Ross and Jill Meyers of the Triton Museum of Art.

From the City of San Jose: Mayor Sam Liccardo and the great team from the office of the Mayor including Communications Director David Low; City of San Jose Chief Business Communications Officer Cara Douglas, Deputy City Manager Kim Walesh and Event Director Tammy Turnipseed; Deputy Chief Michael Knox and the entire San Jose Police Department;

Vicky Day, Rosemary Barnes and the San Jose Airport team; Steve Kirschner of the SAP Center at San Jose; San Jose Sports Authority head honcho Patricia Ernstrom, David Eadie and Carrie Benjamin; San Jose Convention Center's Gabe Nemeth and Matt Reed; and San Jose Earthquakes' David Kaval, Richard Fedesco and Chris Gennuso.

From the City of Oakland: Mayor Libby Schaaf and the fantastic team from the office of the Mayor including Director of Communications Erica Terry Derryck and Director of Equity & Strategic Partnerships Jose Corona; City of Oakland's Special Events lead Jim MacIlvaine; and John Albrecht and the Oakland Airport team.

To the transportation and public transit community with whom our team worked so closely to enable residents and fans to travel safely and as easily as possible around the region. We'd like to thank the great staffs of the following agencies for their tremendous effort and partnership: 311, 511.org, AC Transit, ACE, BAAQMD, Bay Area taxi drivers, BART, Blue & Gold Fleet, California Highway Patrol, Caltrain, Caltrans, Capital Corridor, Clipper, Golden Gate Ferry, Golden Gate Transit, MTC, Mineta San Jose International Airport, Oakland International Airport, SamTrans, San Francisco Bicycle Coalition, San Francisco International Airport, SFMTA, SolTrans, Uber, VTA and WETA, as well as Captain David Lera and the entire Santa Clara County Sheriff's office.

To every community that participated in the 50 Tour and Super Communities initiatives and the people who made it possible for residents to celebrate Super Bowl locally, especially

California Lt. Governor Gavin Newsom; Al Bito of the City of Campbell; Alina Kwak of the City of Fremont; Marc and Brenda Lhormer of the Napa Valley Film Festival; Anne Stedler of City of Pacifica; Tammy Turnipseed of City of San Jose; Sheila Tucker and Jennifer Yamaguma of City of Santa Clara; Julie Myers at the City of Sausalito; Mark Crabb of Sonoma County Tourism and Monica Rodriguez and Katie Young of the Sonoma Harvest Fair; Charlene Lennon of Visit Santa Rosa; Melyssa Laughlin at Visit Vacaville; Joanna Altman of the City of Vallejo; and the team at the Santa Cruz Beach Boardwalk and the Mountain View Art & Wine Festival.

On a personal note, Pat is forever grateful for Bill Campbell, his friend, coach and "secret advisor" for Super Bowl 50 who sadly passed away in April 2016; his brother Mike Gallagher who grew up in the "fun business" too and was always there for him; his wise friend and sounding board Lou Giraudo; former NFL Events chief Jim Steeg for his generosity with Super Bowl historical information; and former SF Travel chair Toni Knorr and David Nadelman for going to bat with the San Francisco hospitality industry to support the Super Bowl 50 bid.

Stephanie is personally grateful for the support of her family and friends throughout the Host Committee journey, especially Lizz Ogletree for delicious home-cooked sustenance; Mimi Towle for short escapes into the Marin hills with Sammy and Lucky; her family for flying out from Boston to be part of the Super Bowl 50 experience; and her husband Mike for not only his incredible support of her work but also for always encouraging her to chase her dreams.

And finally, Pat and Stephanie are thankful to have had this opportunity to work with each other on this book. The "fun business" is certainly more fun when you have a true partner.

CPSIA information can be obtained
at www.ICGtesting.com
Printed in the USA
FSOW03n0909020517
33771FS